"A scaringly honest, gorgeously told story of one woman's awakening from a two-month coma after her baby's birth and her long road back to love and purpose and the rediscovery of who she is. Lyrical and unforgettable."

—**Eric Metaxas,** *New York Times* bestselling author
of *Bonhoeffer: Pastor, Martyr, Prophet, Spy*
and *Amazing Grace: William Wilberforce*
and the Heroic Campaign to End Slavery

"A lyrical, stunning tale of one woman's return to life. A laughing, weeping story of a family finding their way back home."

—**Claire Díaz-Ortiz** leads social innovation at Twitter, Inc.

"O'Connor takes us into the groundlessness of intense trauma and reentry, and candidly (sometimes brutally so), shows what it is to resist, receive, and *be* . . . grace.

—**Laura Munson,** author of the *New York Times* and
international bestseller *This Is Not the Story You Think It Is*

"Be careful picking up *The Long Awakening* because you may be unable to put it down. With clear-eyed intelligence and heart, Lindsey O'Connor succeeds in taking her readers along on her journey through coma, awakening, and an arduous recovery aided by her family and, above all, her loving husband. This is a moving, intimate story, arrestingly written, that glimmers with a keen understanding of what matters."

—**John Biewen,** audio program director at the Center for
Documentary Studies at Duke University,
and editor of *Reality Radio: Telling True Stories in Sound*

"Brilliant and renewing. A spectacular work of reflection, remembering, reconciling, and recovering. Substantial and wonderful. Memoir writing at its finest."

—**Patricia Raybon,** author of *My First White Friend*
and *I Told the Mountain to Move*

"For Lindsey O'Connor, surviving a 47-day coma was only prologue to a miraculous story of science, doubt, faith, and love. Hers is an astonishing narrative, courageously told."

—**David Schulman**, former senior producer BBC Americana and creator of public radio's *Musicians in Their Own Words*

"Good things often happen when a great story meets a talented storyteller. But Lindsey O'Connor's grasp of literary journalism gives this personal narrative much more substance than the typical memoir. Strong reporting places her experience in larger contexts that add depth and understanding. Her writer's eye yields revealing detail and mind-expanding metaphor. Her sense of structure produces a magnetic narrative arc that follows the transformation of both body and mind. And her relentless effort to find meaning in her experience teases insight out of her personal experience while it builds toward the grander themes that help us all live better lives. The result is a complete package, a true *story* in the deepest sense of the word."

—**Jack Hart**, author of *Storycraft,* writing coach, former managing editor of *The Oregonian,* and editor of two Pulitzer Prize–winning stories

The Long Awakening

a memoir

by

Lindsey O'Connor

Revell

a division of Baker Publishing Group
Grand Rapids, Michigan

Published by Revell
a division of Baker Publishing Group
P.O. Box 6287, Grand Rapids, MI 49516-6287
www.revellbooks.com

Printed in the United States of America

Library of Congress Cataloging-in-Publication Data is on file at the Library of Congress, Washington, DC.

ISBN 978-0-8007-1876-3 (cloth)
ISBN 978-0-8007-2317-0 (ITPE)

13 14 15 16 17 18 19   7 6 5 4 3 2

For Caroline Aileen

1

I DO NOT REMEMBER the day, the moment, I first remembered who I was or what was my life.

Before I was pulled back from the deep of a forty-seven-day sleep, before I understood what had happened while I slept or that I had slept at all, before the moment I saw his face leaning close to mine and before the long journey after my waking when I lost my way and myself, I knew where, who, I was. Other things, however, take a season to know.

On a crisp fall day in 2002 the whiteboard on the wall to the left of the sliding glass doors reads "Today is October 15th. Your nurse is Marsha," written with the hasty scrawl of a busy ICU nurse, but I am oblivious.

"Honey?" he says. "Can you hear me?"

Do I hear him? Or am I dreaming his voice?

I don't know what's real or what's not. I'm lying in the black sense-deprived place of preconsciousness, the tiny space between dreaming and waking. But I don't leave. I linger.

I hear muffled sounds, voices, then they fade away into a faint ringing sound that rises like bubbles hitting eardrums as you sink below the surface; I am underwater, floating in the sea of alter-consciousness, bobbing in preawareness, an incorporeal, matter-less, drifting existence.

Days, weeks later I will remember the sunny day when I was sixteen at summer camp in Texas floating down the Alto Frio river. At a sharp bend the flowing water hit a cement embankment. I floated downstream toward it and saw my fellow campers sitting on the sidewalk a few feet above the water's surface. As I reached the wall, before I could grab the edge and hoist myself up, the undercurrent grabbed me, pushed me under. I could see the obscure image of my friends above. Quit fighting, I thought. Let the river sweep me downstream. I'll pop up if I don't fight. I surrendered to the water until my lungs ached. I might die, I thought.

I kick, reach up once more, then a hand reaches into the water, grasps mine, pulls me up. It's unforgettable to see the surface from underwater, the dark below you, light filtering above, trapped in between, floating—don't fight it—then longing to break the surface and breathe, out of the water into life. Like the Alto Frio, like a baby, like a coma, like the watery edges of dreams. On this 2002 autumn day I don't resist. Don't fight it. Until I hear a faraway deep-timbered voice, strong and soft, as familiar to me as my own. A voice that is warmth, a hundred summer days, and I am winter. I am drawn, pulled, to the warmth. Rescued from the depth.

It is this voice that pierces the edges of my waking.

"Honey, can you hear me?" Tim says with an urgency I don't understand, a near excitement. I do. Of course I can hear you, I think. Why wouldn't I?

Then I see him, this man I married, this man I love, moving toward me and bending close, his square jaw, his blue-green eyes, soft, coming into focus. My fingertips inch across wrinkled white sheets, then touch cold metal holding me in bed while wisps of cool air swirl around my neck, foreign and out of place, and a rhythmic mechanical sound whooshes in, out, in, out, inhale, exhale, amidst the smell of plastic and antiseptic.

"Hi, honey!" he says and strokes my hair, eyes locked on mine with a peculiar look on his face, intent, unusual, an expression that looks very much like . . . what? Like . . . devotion. Like the way he'd looked down at me the night we'd said goodbye after our wedding rehearsal dinner. Devotion that says delight and love and joy without a word. It startles me.

It's the kind of look you see in the movies when the hero locks eyes with the heroine from across the room, strides toward her, drawn like a magnet. Before the movie kiss, before the embrace or the passion or declarations of love, the guy gazes at the girl. You sit in the theater putting one kernel of popcorn after another in your mouth until that look and you stop, kernel midair. In your real married life amidst kids and a mortgage and chicken casserole and weed mitigation, you latch on to date night and laugh, make love often enough, and you live your big beautiful ordinary life where in between and after the fights that are also part of your ordinary wonderful life, you feel love like you never imagined at twenty-two or twenty-four. But what's not there, what you've stopped expecting, is "that look" and when you see it onscreen it catches you by surprise and you sort of soundlessly catch your breath.

I look at him now as I wake up. He is gazing at me with that look, with tender eyes and the softest smile, like he hasn't seen me in a million years.

The soft-focus image of him clears as he bends his 6'4" frame down until his face is inches from mine. He's wearing a white buttoned-down shirt. I love that shirt. I love that smell.

"Honey, you can hear me?"

Of course I can hear you. You've woken me up. I nod, waking like it's any other morning in the world, opening my eyes from last night's sleep.

"Don't try to talk," he says. "You're on a ventilator, it's helping you breathe."

I nod in understanding. OK, I have a trach. I absorb this with a matter-of-fact detachment like he'd just told me that it was supposed to be sunny outside today, but instead it was raining, and wasn't that something, to which I'd reply, well, no, it's really not something, it's just rain. That's the way it is. Get out your umbrella, it's raining, how about that, and by the way what's for lunch? I have a trach. I can't talk. A little trach, a little rain. There you have it.

"Honey, do you know where you are? You're in the hospital."

I'm in the hospital. A little rain.

"Honey . . . you've been here forty-seven days."

It will be weeks until I begin to hear the one thing that had been worse for him than watching the ventilator sucking air out and pumping it back in through the hole in my neck, and the chest tubes protruding from each side of my torso, and the gastric tube entering my stomach with nutrition, weeks until I hear the fear he'd been living with for almost two months. The doctors had warned him. Most likely, they'd said, the MRI looks questionable, bad, they'd said; the near bleed out during the birth and consequent oxygen deprivation was a major brain assault, they'd said, and he'd seen it. The signs and responses of a lost woman trapped in her body, a catastrophe that had pushed Tim to the brink of his beliefs, where my life, his life, hung in the balance.

Forty-seven days. Immediately I roll my eyes.

Today is October 15th. Your nurse is Marsha. He sees nothing but my eye roll and in that instant, he knows. He knows in the inexplicable way longtime married couples have of being able to read each other, knowing what the other's about to say, and he knows now that my eye roll means only one thing—"What a week I'm having!" An eye roll at bleak news was our black humor communicated wordlessly over many years, taken from an old Eugene Levy movie where a week of unfortunate events ends with a jab to the thigh of a Novocain hypodermic and he'd walked away dragging a dead leg saying, "What a week I'm having." Tim and I would eye roll at each other at traffic tickets and funeral preparations, a multipurpose silent communication where black humor lets you take the next step.

He sees my eye roll and smiles, a wave of relief washing over his face in an instant. He knows that I'm in there. There will be cause to doubt later, but for now, this moment, he knows. And that is enough to carry him through what lies ahead.

"Honey, we're going to move you to a different hospital today," he says.

"Where?" I mouth.

"To Swedish Medical Center," he says.

"Why?" I ask.

He hesitates. "Because we think they can take better care of you there." That's all he says. He does not explain it's a Level 1 trauma center, or that Swedish is connected to Craig Hospital, the hospital in Denver that treated Superman, the actor Christopher Reeves, the hospital renowned for the neurorehabilitation of traumatic brain injury patients.

He takes my hand looking like someone concerned trying very hard not to look concerned. This simple exchange between us will come back to him over and over to comfort him in the coming days and he will remember he had told me a fact and I had responded with a question. Asking questions is what I do, what I did, what had been my stock-in-trade as a journalist, and just now, hours or so out of a coma, I was asking questions, but more importantly, my question to his statement was an appropriate response. I was tracking with him. For now.

My mind hears him and I absorb this news believing it's true and believing it is not so. I've been here forty-seven days and you are perfectly right and isn't that something, what a week I'm having . . . I really just went to sleep last night.

His caress on my arm and the look in his eyes engulf me.

"Lin, do you remember that you had a baby?" he asks.

The question hangs in the air, heavy, sodden.

A baby. Do I remember that I had a baby? Tick, tick, tick, the gears in my mind rev for a second, two, three, and I ponder this. Did I have a baby?

Was this a dream? In dreams we are not contained by time or space or physics or logic. You are there one minute talking to your pharmacist and in the next instant you are sitting at a sunny piazza, sipping cappuccino with your best friend, commenting how wonderful it is that you are both in Italy, and then you remember that you've left your child at home and, boom,

11

you are at her side without the hassle of airport security, lines, or all that tedious time waiting at gate 43. You have a thought or an experience and then suddenly you are having another and no sense of time passes in between. Bits of dreams, good ones, and single moments in an ordinary day, are like movie trailers with the best parts, the prettiest parts, edited together. We awaken and wonder if this was real, then we wonder what it meant or if it meant anything at all.

I lie in the bed with the metal railings and white wrinkly sheets and the nurse call button I'm unable to press, and roll the word "coma" around my mind like a child. Where am I again? What's happened to me? Who am I?

I look at Tim and see Brent Kinman, our friend and pastor, standing next to him. I notice his blue cap with white letters that pops with color in this white world, and his smile, both soft and intense, like he's seeing something he can't quite believe.

"Tim," he says, "why don't you tell her her story?"

Tim leans over the stainless steel railing of the bed on the second floor in the ICU and bends close. His eyes smile and his brow furrows.

Did I? Did I remember I had a baby?

2

I'D LAIN IN THE DEEP, within the mystery of consciousness, a place of nothingness, of dreams, dreams, dreams, a place without time until I felt and heard those hundred summer days.

Weeks later I will remember another voice, different from the warmth that had penetrated my darkness with startling clarity.

"Mommy!" I heard with the muffled sound one hears when floating near the surface of a lake, water against eardrums; I heard her without seeing her and blurred images come and go, but the voice rang true, high-pitched, joyful. My child. She's excited. Calling me.

There were no thoughts of, Oh, I've got to sit up and talk to her. What is she doing? How is she? No thoughts of, Oh, it's Alli, my youngest child, my nine-year-old; I'm so glad she's here.

Just My Child. Excited. Calling me. Her voice, crystal and steel, sank into the world I was in from the world above me just out of my reach, a world I wanted.

"Mommy! Hi, Mommy!"

"Alli," Tim said. "Go get Mommy's glasses."

I heard her footsteps running out the door. Then more darkness, sleep, until Tim put my glasses on my face.

"Here. Is that better? Can you see now?" I focused hard and

saw his face and her chestnut hair bobbing up and down and I nod, worlds touching until sleep takes me again.

Today is October 15th. Your nurse is Marsha. Whoosh, whoosh, whoosh. Think. Think. Tim's waiting for an answer. Do I remember?
Yes. I had a baby last night. I did.
A little girl. And I got to hold her.
Five minutes. Just five minutes.

I nod to Tim. Yes, I remember I had a baby. Relief washes over his face and he smiles and looks like he might cry. Why, why did he look like that?

There had been a decade between our youngest child and this one, and she'd been no surprise. Choosing to have this baby at forty, nine years after our fourth child's birth, was an enigma. I'd worked for years reporting and writing, story after story. This, I'd think while working on a piece, is my little place in the world. I loved being a journalist, and I also loved being a mother. A few months before this pregnancy I'd read a *Wall Street Journal* article about a trend of growing numbers of women wanting a baby for their fortieth birthday for many different reasons, but lots of people hear about a woman having a midlife "caboose" and figure you have a new husband, you had an "oops," or you were crazy. Many decisions in life are made for multiple reasons and sometimes why we do what we do isn't completely understood, even to ourselves, maybe especially to ourselves. Radical or not, Tim and I sensed our family was supposed to be one person bigger.

When I first held her in my arms I'd leaned my cheek on her pink-and-blue-striped stocking cap and cradled her chest and chin in my hand.

"Smile, hon," Tim had said. Snap. "That was a good one." He'd captured the first minutes of our acquaintance. I was content to hold her swaddled in her receiving blanket, my hand on her tiny round rump, feeling her seven and something pounds. There would be time later for the unwrapping, the inspection of newborn fingers and toes and the small of her back. Time later.

Five minutes. Just five minutes.

Velvety baby cheek on my chest, the feel of those five minutes, is what I remembered later, when I first remembered her, what I remember still.

The memory of the searing pain of a uterine rupture has stayed with me, an amber molten steel rod lodged in my abdomen. When they'd wheeled me out of the birthing room into the corridor for emergency surgery, I'd looked up at the nurses and anesthesiologist injecting Diprivan into my IV, he on one side of the gurney, nurses on the other, and said, "Please take care of me. I have five children now," then the sedative surged. Darkness began. How could I know, how could I possibly know those were my last spoken words for almost three months? But then life doesn't seem to give us advance warning of abrupt turns.

Please take care of me. Five children.

Those hundred summer days to my winter draws me, pulls me with the sense of his presence first, then like tuning in a barely audible radio station, finding it and turning up the volume, I hear him.

The voices, mine, then his, August 30th and October 15th, are back-to-back audio cuts seamlessly edited together with time in the middle erased.

Please take care of me. I have five children now.

A hundred summer days.

Honey, can you hear me?

The cool air encircles my neck in time to the whoosh, whoosh, whoosh of the machine next to me. Today is October 15th. Your nurse is Marsha. If I've been here forty-seven days, what about my baby? Is she . . . dead? A chill shivers through me. The heart of a mother beats for her child until it beats no more. "Is she OK?" I mouth.

"Yes! She's fine," he says, quick to relieve me. "She's beautiful and healthy. Jacquelyn's bringing her up in a little while, they're on their way." He tells me I've been in a medically induced coma to allow my body, brain, and lungs time to heal, that's why I've been here forty-seven days.

"Honey, after she was born you had two emergency surgeries that night and they had to do a hysterectomy. I'm so sorry." He looks at me, sadness in his eyes, like he expects me to burst into tears at the news. Why does this matter? Uterus in, uterus out. A little rain. Get out your umbrella. I had no use for that body part anymore. Should I be upset about this? Weeks later a nurse will come in and ask, "Was the hysterectomy done abdominally?" Hmmm. I lift the covers and look at my stomach. No, I look up at her and shake my head. I hadn't had an abdominal incision. However I discover later that I had; I'd slept so long that by the time I'd awakened and looked, my abdominal incision had healed.

Exerted and medicated I drift off and awaken again, the morning's clarity fogged, and am mystified by a room full of people. It's a party.

Why am I at a party in my pajamas? I blink. My children are there, my stepsister Donna, my best friend Kathy, Tim, and nurses, all milling about talking with each other, smiling, smiling, laughing, about . . . something I should know. I remember I can't speak so I don't even try to communicate that I'm sorry, but I'm not sure why you're all here.

Kathy walks over to me looking like she won the lottery and she holds Caroline up to me. I shrug. How can she be mine? How can that baby be mine? She is, but how? I just had a baby and she is too big to be mine.

Again I sleep. I wake and Tim and I are now alone. If this direct air-conditioning vent blowing on my neck would stop, I'll get up. Yes, I'm going to get up. Drugs, coma, forty-seven days. OK. I'm just going to get up now. I move, but go nowhere.

He has so many questions. How do I feel? Do I hurt? Can he get me anything? Do I understand what he's told me? What am I trying to say to him? He leans close and I smell his scent of starched cotton and familiar flesh that is distinctly him, that I love, and I try hard to form the words clearly so he can read my lips. How did this happen? Why did this happen? What is happening today? I can't make him understand my questions. His eyes narrow, he purses his lips, leans even closer, looking only at my mouth. He starts to answer. No, that isn't the question. I shake my head and try again. Hit. I nod. Miss. And so it goes until I shake my head and close my eyes.

Where had I been? I'd been elsewhere and then I was found. As so often happens, a moment, or a series of moments, the bat of an eye instantly changes everything, takes us somewhere we don't want to go and leaves us some place other, a place where our life is shoved into some foreign shape, a place where love goes missing, its meaning eludes, and we are a self gone missing, an identity lost. A place where we don't even recognize who we are.

I am desperate to become un-lost, to find all that's missing.

The fog returns. We wait for the ambulance, and wait and wait and I am like a little girl with her suitcase packed and waiting by the door, waiting for the signal that it's time to actually leave for Grandma's or vacation or somewhere that is safe and fun and better than here, waiting for the all clear that her suitcase can be put in the trunk and she can begin traveling, anticipation becoming action. We wait for hours. Then finally two men in blue come into my room, nurses move me to a portable ventilator. Clank, they check that the metal rails on the bed, which have been constantly up, are secure. Chest tubes, IV tubes, catheter tubes, ventilator tubes, feeding tubes are all checked and rechecked and draped over me, carefully organizing the spaghetti of life support. Then we are moving.

"I'm right here, honey. I'm going with you," he says, which we've been over. A couple of times.

"You're coming?" I'd asked earlier.

"Oh yeah. They should be here soon."

"When?"

"They say it'll be any minute."

"You're coming?"

He reassures me again, and now that my bed was moving I ask again. Same answer.

"I'm right behind you," he says. The bed moves through the door into the corridor, Tim follows and I feel thrilled and scared and have no idea why except that it is time to put my suitcase in the trunk.

I'm excited, I'm traveling, and my heart pounds. I think it very odd and comforting that they have put me in the back of a station wagon instead of an ambulance. The double doors in the back are open and I've been put in headfirst, feet near the doors, which is so thoughtful of them because I can see out the back window at all the places we've just been, like I did when I was a kid sitting on the rear-facing seat of our old blue Ford station wagon. Tim stands in the open back doors, waiting, talking to me, talking to the nurse.

Get in, I think. There's plenty of room. That nurse will move and you can sit right next to me. Turn around and face the back like me and this will be kind of fun, we can see out the back together. He talks to the nurse. My heart is all skittery. Travel is exciting. I think I might be scared, but I'm not sure. No, I am scared. Pretty sure of it. And I'm excited. Little bit scared, lot excited. Then more scared. But why? If Tim would only get in the back of this station wagon we could get going. Get in already. We are not moving. The nurse is taking my vitals, heart rate, blood pressure. The nurse seems to be the one holding up the show and I begin to wonder if the driver's getting irritated yet sitting all at the ready behind the wheel. Why won't Tim get in the car?

"Honey, we need you to calm down," he says, leaning into the back, patting my legs. The nurse is at my side near my head and she seems so busy. How strange that I am angled in the back of this station wagon. How did they do that with the seats? Our station wagon when I was a kid had that old bench seat facing the rear. Some had those seats on either side, didn't they? So I'm not quite sure how I am in here at an angle, looking out the back, head near the car's driver side, feet near the passenger side.

"Can you calm down, Lindsey?" the nurse says with warmth and firmness, not a question at all. Tim still doesn't get in and I feel like tapping my foot, being all at the ready, the driver and me.

"Lin, I know you're scared, but try to . . ."

My heart is pounding now, indefinable distress flows through me. I will be fine if we would just start the car, get going.

"Her heart's racing," I hear the nurse tell Tim. You know things are off when people start talking about you in third person. I am getting tired, and irritated, and agitated, and pound, pound, pound, my heartbeats speed up again until I can feel them in my temples, vibrating my chest. Fear spreads through me, like sudden hot rain.

"Her heart rate is 152," the nurse tells Tim. Third person again.

"Can I ride with her?" he asks the nurse.

"Not now," she answers.

"OK, I'll follow you. I'm in that gray Range Rover."

They talk to each other in hurried, urgent tones. . . . just follow . . . leaving now . . . her heart . . . have to give her . . .

"Honey!" he shouts and I jerk my eyes open, the slate edges of all that's around me receding and the golden-red trees and Tim's white shirt against the aquamarine sky, the gray panels of the inside of the station wagon, come back into focus and I see his face, his blue-green eyes, looking at me and I lock onto them.

"I can't ride with you," he says, "but I'm going to be right behind you. I'll follow you all the way and I'll be there when you get out. Can you calm down for me? They need to give you something to help you . . . some medicine . . . got to slow down your heart . . ."

"Lin!"

I open my eyes, and concentrate on slowing my heart and

willing my veins to push out the sedative and the fear. I'm not going back there, that place of other I've just left. Fight. Rise above this.

I look at him and mouth, "I'm scared."

"I know, honey. I know," he says leaning in enough to touch my hand. "I'll see you there," he says as the nurse injects liquid stillness into my IV.

Why won't they let him come with me? Why am I afraid? I want to just ride with him. Maybe they'll let me do that. I like his car. We can move my suitcase.

"I love you," he says. The double doors close and I see his face through the window until we drive away and I see nothing but sky, then nothing at all. He is gone and I am gone.

On the other side of those doors Tim looks at me through the glass until the ambulance pulls away and he turns walking fast over fallen leaves as he hurries to his car. He follows the ambulance questioning if he made the right decision to move me to the other hospital, terrified by my deteriorating vital signs. What if I've killed her? he wonders. This was the second time that he'd agonized that his decision would cause my death. Who could imagine that one could ever wonder that about their loved one? But August 30th had changed everything.

It had been the day our baby had come into the world and I had left, a day that had begun so normally and ended so utterly not, a day that had begun all smiles and excitement and anticipation and joy and ended with running and panic and blood and tears.

3

THE DAY THAT CHANGED EVERYTHING had begun a season ago, before the red and gold aspen leaves fell to the grass and browned and crisped and collected against the curbs, back when the verdant leaves held tightly and fluttered in the hot summer breeze.

In a black leather journal he recorded the day beauty turned ugly.

> *Friday, August 30th, 2002*
> *3:00 AM*
> *I'm awake, which given the time is extremely unusual for me as I am such a sound sleeper. Lin is returning to bed from the bathroom. I speak to her—"Is anything wrong?"*
> *She replies, "We're going to have a baby today!"*
> *"How do you know?" I say.*
> *Reply—"My water broke." That's not happened with any other of our four previous pregnancies. She comes back to bed and we begin to time the contractions. About an hour or so goes by—just lying there, talking, timing. We finally get up to shower and dress for the trip.*

Neither of us thought about what I'd said two days earlier.
"You know, Tim, some women still die in childbirth."

21

He'd scowled. "No Lin . . ."
"Well, not very often," I'd said, "but it happens."

5:30 AM
   *We depart for the hospital. Contractions are about six
   minutes apart and fairly strong.*

7:30–8:00 AM
   *Epidural is in and taking effect. She is a new woman.
   And we wait.*

11:00 AM
   *Dilation five to six centimeters. I leave to make a phone
   call, get a bite and gas up the car.*

———

This wasn't the first time he'd ducked and covered during a delivery, not that he'd ever planned it, it just sort of crept up on him. During the labor of our second child, Katherine-Claire, when I'd hit a high-tension episode resulting from an ineffective epidural, I'd had to send a nurse on a search and rescue mission to retrieve him. He'd fallen asleep on a waiting room couch. He was the type of guy who would have been more at home in the previous generation when husbands stayed in waiting rooms fidgeting with magazines, drinking vending machine coffee, pacing or going out for a smoke until the all clear was given that they'd had a son or daughter and then and only then would they enter the fierce scene where birth had occurred. But through the years and through our children's births he'd dutifully taken his place alongside me in Labor and Delivery, answering the doctor politely every time, that No thank you, he would not care to cut the cord, when his inclination was to shout, "Are you out of your mind?" Occasional moments of being MIA during labor was his answer to his misfortune of having become a father in such a progressive time.

Once he sprained his ankle on the basketball court so bad

it turned black and swelled to the size of a cantaloupe, but he just got a Vicodin and leg boot from the doctor and came home to work his crossword puzzle like he'd only stubbed a toe, and he could push numbers around at his office for sixty, seventy hours a week for months on end, years maybe, without a complaint. "Suck it up," he'd tell me. There were only a few times he couldn't do this himself, like when one of our kids would wiggle their tooth, "Daddy pull it," and he'd grimace and look away, or in the emergency room with our child needing stitches where he'd sit across the room with his color drained, and of course, during childbirth.

One thing he had going for him on August 30th when he inadvertently ditched me was his uncanny ability to disarm me and make me laugh while I'm recovering from rage at him, a phenomenon I don't understand and have no choice but to let him milk for all its worth, one that has held us in good stead these two decades. Walking into the birthing room after nearly missing the birth of this last child would have been a keen time to have rolled my eyes dramatically and say, "What a week I'm having!" He knew that line would have gotten him out of the doghouse today.

12:30 PM
I arrive back at the room not realizing that I've been gone an hour and a half. Lin is upset, fearful that she might have to deliver with me gone. The dilation has been quicker than the one centimeter per hour told to us by the nurse. She is about nine to ten centimeters. I apologize and comfort my wife. I'm such an idiot.

1:00 PM
The troops assemble in the room as the time to push has arrived.

1:38 PM
Caroline Aileen O'Connor is delivered. Blood is suctioned

from the baby's mouth. At some point later a tube is inserted
into the baby's stomach to remove additional blood that
was swallowed.
I busy myself with the baby while the doctor attends
to my wife.

An hour or so later our other children arrive and Tim holds
Caroline up while they look starry-eyed at their new sister. Our
eldest child, Jacquelyn, three weeks into her freshman year in
college, takes the baby into her arms. "She's beautiful. She's so
beautiful," she says, as if taken by surprise that she could be so
quickly captivated. Fifteen-year-old Katherine-Claire (who'd
long since become "Claire" to us) decided to stay home to clean
the house, which was a free pass to avoid the hospital. Allison,
looking like the quintessential little girl nearing the end of her
single-digit years, in a baby pink T-shirt and long chestnut hair
ponytailed in a loose bun, hovers over the baby. Collin, in a yellow print shirt and buzz haircut, looks particularly neat for a
twelve-year-old boy and smiles with uncharacteristic timidity.
They're little bees buzzing over the delicate flower swaddled in
pink and white.

About 3:00 PM
We are now alone—I hold the baby, talk to Lin when
she just lays back and stops talking to me—she is notice-
ably pale.

If we had known those moments were the end of the beginning would Tim and I have changed a thing? Maybe I'd have
traced the curve of her cheek with my finger and held her close
breathing her in for another minute or two or five. After the
crowd at the birth had faded and he and I were alone with our
daughter, would I have memorized the words we said to each
other in those soft moments and held them sacred as he held
her? Pay attention we'd say, record this we'd say, these moments
won't come this way again. I wish I could have pushed hard

against the pain and the pallor and wrenched a snatch more of time, precious time, but now my ears ring and his voice fades, the moment fades, and I'm powerless to stop it. The obstetrician returns and snaps on gloves, "Hemorrhaging . . . surgery now . . . ," she says with staccato words and asks for an oral consent, all hurrying, all urgency.

I affirmed the consent then look at my frightened, frail wife, best friend, grab her hand and pray.

Tim watches them roll the gurney down the long hall with the sound of rubber wheels on polished flooring and then the operating suite doors swing closed and he stands alone, still. It was just yesterday, that summer before our college classes resumed, that we'd strolled the San Antonio River Walk watching moonlight glitter on the water like a blanket of stars descended from the heavens, saying look, this beauty comes for you, now, later.

How could it be almost twenty years since we'd stood at an altar under the candlelight of love and bliss and untarnished hope? "I, Lindsey, take you, Timothy, to be my lawful husband, to love, honor . . ." Then he slid the gold band on my finger. "I, Timothy, take you, Lindsey . . . in sickness and in health, till death do us part."

He walks to the surgery waiting room around the corner and is soon joined by our eldest daughter Jacquelyn, and Brent. They sit in uncomfortable chairs and wait in the room where that is what you do and where no one thumbs through magazines and everyone tries to ignore the TV. Hours later the surgery is over and the recovery room is a stop on the way to ICU and then down again to the operating room. "Code White," they hear over the PA unaware this is the call summoning available staff to the medical emergency of a hemorrhaging patient. I had no idea of course, nor him, that I was bleeding out. If I had, if I'd been able, I'd have hit rewind, drawn back every unit of life force leaving me, to spare my family of what was to come.

Later that night a second emergency surgery was needed.

Tim and Brent follow the gurney on the way to the OR. A nurse turns to Tim while they walk. "Here, you'll want this," she says and hands him a plastic specimen cup. He looks into it and sees the gold wedding band and diamond engagement ring with a chunk out of both. "We had to cut them off," she says.

He watches them go into the patient elevator, then he turns for the public elevator, steps in and as the doors close he stares at the rings and the gap in the gold. With this ring I thee wed. The tokens of that bond, broken, in the bottom of a urine cup.

More Code White. People run toward the OR with units of blood. A chaplain comes into the waiting room to talk to Tim. "That's kind of odd," Tim said to Brent after he'd left. "We didn't call for a chaplain."

When the nurse supervisor enters the waiting room with an update she says, "I have to tell you, now it's critical," and she explains the hematocrit—percentage of red blood cells, thus oxygen, in the blood. "A normal person's is around forty. Lindsey's is five. But," she added, "we think she'll make it off the table."

Tim and Brent and Jacquelyn look at each other, then back at her.

"Where is her mother?" the nurse asks Tim. "Have you notified her next of kin?"

"Her mother is deceased and her dad and stepmom live out of state. I'm all she's got."

At two a.m. with the second surgery over, a cot has been brought into the ICU room so he can sleep in the same room with me. The children are scattered: Jacquelyn sleeps in the waiting room, Claire has been picked up from the house by our friends Coletta and Craig Smith, and Collin and Allison went home with my friend Carol MacKey after she'd come to see the baby. Having the children in the care of longtime friends gave Tim a small measure of comfort that they have not been lost in the frightening madness. He's been awake now for almost twenty-four hours and traumatized like a bystander witnessing a car crash. Just that morning he'd driven me here, both of us vibrant with the expectant joy of a new life coming, and now he wasn't even able to communicate that he was next to me, and I couldn't respond to him, squeeze his hand, or tell him that I knew he was there, which I didn't. Get out of the bed, climb into his, and hold him tight. If only. He collapses onto the cot and in the quiet of the night with nothing now to distract him, he contemplates what's just happened, then as silently as he can, he cries.

4

WASN'T IT JUST YESTERDAY, a minute ago, that we had been young? Tim and I had sat on a dock that summer afternoon as the hot Houston sun faded. I'd slipped into the lake and swam a few yards, then turned and looked back at him, and we laughed the way two people falling in love do, him smiling down at me from the dock, me looking up at him, buoyant in twilight's darkening water.

He'd asked my father's permission to marry me before I saw the ring in the box, and he won my mother over from the start, theirs being a mutual affinity and rapport. I'd told him all kinds of stories about her from when I was a young child, days when the sound of my mother's voice had magnetized me. She'd call my name and I was at her side and felt moored, safe. Laying my head on her chest I'd listen to her breathe and feel her heart beating through mine. She was mine, and until my brother Paul was born seven years after me, I was only hers. She was a mother who played with me. One afternoon when I was five, in the little white house on Euclid Street, we lay on her bed, her propped on one elbow with her arm over me, her voice soft as a cloud, singing "Anything You Can Do" and I'd sing back that she couldn't do anything better than me, then she'd tickle me and we'd laugh.

Home to me was wrapped up in her as we were wrapped in a story. Long before I was old enough to ask her to read me a book she was doing so, so I can't recall life without books, without stories. "Go, dog, go" she'd say and ask me if I liked green eggs and ham. "Again, Mommy, read it again," and she would and then another and another. But the book that captivated me and connected me to my mother, told me who I was in her world and she in mine, first told me who I was, was a simple book with a turquoise cover. She'd pull me onto her lap, "Are you my mother?" she'd read, and tell me about an unfortunate bird who falls out of his nest while his mother is away.

"Mother, mother, where are you?" the bird asked and he searched page after page. I'd look at the bird and look up at my mother, breathe in her scent of laundry soap and White Shoulders, unable to imagine not knowing where your mother was. I listened to her tell of a baby bird who awoke alone in his nest and looked for what was lost, yet the end always came, the mother returned, and her baby was lost no more, until the next time we opened the book. In this story time I knew she was mine and I was hers; I was her bird who'd always be found. Behind the turquoise cover, wrapped in her arms, I also became lost in the power of a beginning, a middle, and an end, a place where the world receded and story filled its space, where I first felt an unidentifiable longing, the wisp of the sense that this story space lay in me, needed out of me.

After she closed the books and put the dogs and Sam and the birdie back on the shelf, she'd pull up the covers and turn off the light. In the way of mothers for centuries she'd say, "Now I lay me down to sleep, I pray the Lord my soul to keep," which comforted me as a child alone in the dark with all my books on the shelf and my mother about to turn and close the door. It was the next part though that made me shudder and lie still as a stone. If I should die, before I wake, I pray the Lord my soul to take. Every time we prayed this I was torn between the comfort and the fear; my soul is being kept, and there could be death before waking.

My parents gave me a childhood of candles on cupcakes, of picnics in parks, of seals at the zoo, of skating and sledding and steaming chocolate poured from our red plaid thermos; of chores and Sunday with hard wooden pews and other things that would set a child out right in the world, make them feel they are rock solid, attached and loved. My father laughed easily and often and I never knew a time when he didn't make me feel wanted and special, worthy of his time, and the best thing he ever gave me in my life, besides the white jewelry box with orange and pink flowers and a ballerina that pirouetted on turquoise silk, was the knowledge that he believed in me.

The year I was thirteen, however, I learned to yell and slam doors and give the silent treatment, and I thought I might drive my mother to the brink of herself and all things civilized. When I turned fourteen she and I had never been so glad to be rid of a year. That said, years later she gave me a crimson bookmark with a poem about having a daughter, her "bright and shining star."

"Try it, you can do it," they'd tell me and I would because knowing that someone thinks you can is the difference between the doing and the not.

When I showed them the story in fourth grade that I wrote they smiled and stuck it in a scrapbook, they came to my speech in the eighth grade, they saw me off for college, then off into the world armed with words and ideas and a journalism degree and a passion to use all three. A beginning, a middle, and an end; it was in me, it was me.

A few years later after I'd gotten my first job at a small television station and moved on to my second I found myself writing wire copy in the Houston City Hall pressroom which terrified me and thrilled me. One day I had to cover a city water project story, a subject which glazed over my eyes. This wasn't new. At the television station I'd written and anchored newscasts, exciting work, but something was missing and I wasn't sure what. A kind older woman who worked in the office had asked me, "If you could do anything in this industry what would you choose?"

"More of what I did after Hurricane Alicia," I said. A col-

league of mine had held a camera while he crouched in a helicopter getting aerial shots of the devastation then rushed back
to edit tape, write, and get the story on the air. But not me. After
the news broke and we did our in-studio jobs, the floodwaters
began to recede and people had stories to tell. For several days I
got to ignore the news cycle and talk to these people and gather
their stories as they told what had happened in their house or
car or yard or office when the monster storm hit, how they rode
it through, the mess and the loss and the hope they faced afterward. Their stories riveted me. A beginning, a middle, and an
end. Real people telling real stories of what it was like to be them.

So, the day of the water project assignment I left the City
Hall pressroom and headed for Lake Houston where the other
reporters and I got on a boat with a Public Works official to
cover the story. I clutched my press packet and noticed how
the papers whipped in the wind, how the boat sounded on the
water that day, what it felt like to be moving across the water
that the city drank. When we got back I tried not to worry that
my colleagues who were all older and more experienced than
me were going to create important stories probably filled with
concepts or angles I didn't fully understand, so what did I know?
Instead I wrote it the way I experienced it, the visceral and real
and human amidst the facts. (These were long before the days
I'd heard the term *narrative journalism*.) Try it. You can do it.
My palms were sweaty as I filed it. My colleagues were going
to see this. I'd sort of bucked the expected way of doing things.
What if I'd made a fool of myself, attempted something and
failed so miserably that others saw foolishness, or found me to
be a fraud? I took a deep breath and did it anyway.

The next morning a colleague walked into the pressroom;
he held my copy. "I saw your story this morning," he said. I
tensed my stomach and shook my foot under the table. "It was
. . . interesting." There. I'd done it. You put yourself out there
and flow upstream and, bam, you pay. "It was different, colorful
. . . it was good," he said. Relief dripped out of me, at least one
person didn't find me lacking, but the best thing: I realized doing

what was truest to me was worth the risk of failure. Beginning, middle, and end.

So, I kept writing stories, and eventually I became a mother, a woman carrying consuming baby love, ambition, and love for a man in one heart.

The first few days after our trauma shattered the beautiful and normal, and unraveled every thread of the sense of control in life, which is really just an illusion we discover at the unraveling, Tim did all you can do at a trauma's shattering—take a step, and then another.

He walked into ICU, greeted the nurse just outside my room, and asked, "Well, how's she doing?"

"Fine," the nurse said.

"Fine?" he shot back. "Fine? What do you mean fine? She walked in here, healthy, under her own power, a week and a half ago to deliver a baby and now she's lying in that bed in a coma in ICU and you tell me she's fine?" He gritted his teeth and waited for an answer.

"Let me get someone you can talk to," the nurse said.

He hadn't realized until now that his need for answers had been masked by the need to just do the next thing, show up and see what today holds. A caseworker came out within minutes and introduced herself. She worked as the liaison between a patient's loved ones and the health care professionals providing treatment.

"My wife's been in the hospital a week and a half and I don't even know what's wrong with her! Why is she on a ventilator? Why is she in a coma? Why does she need a machine to breathe?" he vented. He had so many questions and felt there was never an opportunity to ask them, let alone get feedback from the growing number of specialists who were treating me.

The caseworker listened patiently and told him he didn't have to be in an information vacuum and asked him if it would be helpful if she arranged an all-hands-on meeting, an open forum where all of the health providers treating his wife would meet with him in a room and he could ask all the questions he wanted.

"That's a fantastic idea. When can we do it?" he asked. It was set for two days later.

By 7:45 a.m. everyone filed into the conference room and took their seats, a jambalaya of advanced medical specialties: the obstetrician, pulmonologist, neurologist, the in-charge nurse, and the patient liaison; along with Tim's invitees—my other best friend Susan Wilkinson, my dad and stepmom, and Brent, our pastor. Tim pulled out his black portfolio and began, simply, and to the point.

"What is wrong with my wife?"

They explained that they were dealing with issues stemming from oxygen deprivation the night of the surgeries. They thought there was some manner of brain injury and there was a lung injury and they didn't know why, but mechanical ventilation was still required.

"So," Tim said, "if you were to turn off the ventilator, would my wife die?"

"Yes, she would."

But why had there been a deprivation of oxygen in the blood? Someone explained again about the hematocrit, the measurement of red blood cells (the ones carrying oxygen). He'd heard them tell him the night of the surgeries that mine had fallen to five instead of near forty like normal, but now the significance of that began to dawn. There'd been massive oxygen deprivation because there'd been massive blood loss. Catastrophic blood loss. I had received twenty units of blood and blood products that night, twice the volume of blood in a person's body.

"Well, no wonder! No wonder she's laying up there with a brain injury," said Tim.

Susan reached over and tried to get Tim's attention without anyone noticing, so she grabbed his knee under the table and squeezed. Please be calm, she thought, oh God please let him be calm. He glanced at her, breathed a barely audible "OK," and took a deep breath.

The questions and answers continued around the table.

They had put me in a drug-induced coma—a state of deep unconsciousness induced through a barbiturate like phenobarbital or a sedative like propofol, making a patient unresponsive to external stimuli such as light, pain, noise, and the human voice. The point is to slow the metabolism of the brain and allow it and the body to rest and recover from trauma. The procedure slows the electrical activity of the brain, in some cases, almost to a stop. It can skirt the edges of brain death in order to save life and function.

The difference between a medically induced coma and one brought on by trauma or disease like a stroke is that the induced coma is technically reversible—if the patient lives—but to my family's side of it watching me, and to my side unconscious, the source was irrelevant; the effects were the same.

The multidisciplinary team providing critical care was still trying to pin down what was wrong. Tim wouldn't learn until sometime after this conference that the monster that nearly killed me, repeatedly, and that changed my life was ARDS, acute respiratory distress syndrome—a life-threatening lung injury where the alveoli fill with fluid and the lungs can't do their job of getting oxygen into the blood. They shut down. He'd never heard of this condition but neither have most people, despite the fact that about 150,000 people a year get ARDS and it has numerous complications including multi-organ failure—and that it kills so many. I now know that the mortality rate has dropped to about 40 percent, but at the time half the people with ARDS died, and factoring in the number of complications I had, the death rate was closer to 85 percent.

When the conference ended Tim and Susan sat at the table after everyone had left. Information is always better than the dark and the fear of the unknown. One thing the neurologist had said still hung in the air. "We won't know anything until they can assess her when she's out of the drug-induced coma and conscious," but . . . a recent brain scan had shown "no signs of higher level brain function."

One afternoon Tim dragged himself upstairs to our bedroom after a day and night at the hospital and lay down on our bed exhausted, wrung out emotionally and mentally. He lay there a few moments then opened his eyes. He had to focus. What was it he needed to do? Call Aunt Linda, my aunt, and tell her the bad news, and take a shower. That's all his tired mind could hold, just two things.

After the call and shower he picked up his red jacket from the back of the chair, ready to drive back to the hospital, but he paused, stuck his hand in his coat pocket, and pulled out the specimen jar. He looked at the rings again in the bottom of the cup, shook it, and the metal plunked against the plastic with a hollowness. He opened the top drawer of his highboy dresser, lifted his undershirts covering the small tray that held watches, a honeymoon picture, a silver dollar worn smooth from years in his pocket, and he buried the cup.

5

THEY TELL ME Caroline seemed not to care that the ICU waiting room was partly where she lived. Relatives and friends would gather around the quiet, contented baby and say, "Oh, isn't she beautiful," and sort of catch their breath again because Caroline was a reminder of all that was wrong. She was the contrast in this life-supporting, soul-killing place; it wasn't raw and painful because I was hooked up to machines, the mess was raw and painful because I was hooked up to machines while a newborn baby had need of me.

One afternoon, my oldest daughter, Jacquelyn, left ICU and rode the elevator upstairs to the nursery and took a three-ounce bottle of infant formula from a nurse, removed the canned lid, and screwed on the nipple. She took the wrapped bundle of Caroline into her arms and settled into a rocking chair in the room dimmed for sleeping babies, and gently rocked and fed her baby sister. The next day, she did it again.

My family was their own solar system. Claire, Collin, and Allison floated among family friends, Tim orbited around me, and Jacquelyn orbited around Tim. Everyone I loved in my life was trying to figure out what to do with this baby. Kathy went to my house after they brought Caroline home from the hospital and Jacquelyn had gone back to school. She wanted to care for Caroline until I could, as long as that would take, but for now she had her own family waiting for her, so what next? A plan evolved. When Susan arrived she would relieve Kathy and stay ten days, and then my friend from Houston, Brenda Koinis, would come and Susan would go home. They had enacted the moms-in-residence plan.

During that first week at our house with the baby, Kathy answered the phone constantly. Friends called with concern and offered help; some called almost expressing condolences. Then flowers started coming, meals began to flood in from our church and neighbors, some from people we'd never even met, and then baby gifts began arriving, so Kathy sat down at the kitchen phone desk, pulled a notebook out of the drawer, and quickly created a system to keep track of it all. Heaviness shrouded the home. "This is eerie," Kathy would tell me later, "the way a house feels in between a death and a funeral."

My other best friend, Susan, came next. It was a shame these friends were in my home and I was missing what I'd have thought of as a party if I'd been there. Susan's particular skills parsing medical fact and navigating hospital life, both from innate ability and experience, hard-won from losing her late husband to a lengthy illness, took a backseat to pressing practicalities, like stocking the freezer. "Every day there's a meal from church," she told the kids, amazed. "Every day. Every day there's something," so she served those, then cooked and froze entrees for future days, cooked with the kids, with a pinch of fun during the cooking. The stove was no longer cold.

She also threw a few smiles in the freezer for later. She filled a plastic container with sausage and wild rice casserole and wrote on the label, "Thaw this out. Duh. Put it in the oven on 375 then call me up and tell me it's the best thing you ever ate." The hamburger soup label said, "If you don't like this one, Aunt Kathy made it."

At night Susan took the two a.m. feedings, that unrelenting epitome of life with a newborn, but instead of producing sleep deprivation and joy, fatigue and bonding, it brought Susan sleep deprivation and sadness, fatigue and guilt.

She pulled Caroline into the bed with her, cradled her, put the bottle in her mouth while Caroline made tiny sucking sounds. I have to be your mommy right now, she thought, and a wave a grief washed over her. What would Lin want me to do? I have to enjoy Caroline for Lindsey. She's going to ask me about Caroline when she wakes up. She's going to wake up in a few days and I'm going to feel guilty that I've been taking care of her baby, that I get to be the one cuddling, satisfying the needs of a days-old child, holding her close in the night. I feel like I'm stealing what's hers.

"Hi, baby," she cooed. "You slept pretty good." She tipped the bottle up slightly and looked at her in the dark room, smelled her newborn smell. "Oh . . . your mommy would love to be here. I can't wait for you to see her."

Susan tried to take it all in, every detail, every nuance, to be able to tell me later, but even as she studied Caroline she struggled with how could she tell me how this baby feels? How she was ever going to be able to tell me how this baby smells?

The moms-in-residence plan was not a long-term solution, so Kathy took the baby to her house. My closest friends were torn up that the baby wasn't at home with her family where she belonged, but they questioned how Tim and the kids could possibly take care of her. So Kathy decided she would help—for a weekend, a week, years if needed. She was prepared, excited even, to help raise my child, birth to kindergarten, to mother in my stead. I marvel at the depth of friendship and character that propelled my best friend to do such a thing, a lay-down-your-life act of love.

Tim and my friends and family did their best to wrap themselves around each of the five children, but families are complicated entities.

While Claire instinctively mothered Allison and Collin with

sweet-voiced, pet-name calling tenderness, and Jacquelyn did this with Caroline, Jacquelyn could slip into her overbearing eldest child demeanor with her other siblings, which along with her in-charge status of the home that included them, sometimes brought out old "you're not the boss of me" baggage. Once or twice Tim feared a possible mutiny.

One of my sister-friends, Becky Johnson, came to help with the children, and Allison circled her like a kitten purring for affection. Collin made up a card game for everyone to play, and Becky played one-on-one with him. She looked through pictures with them of me looking whole and normal, and took them to IHop with an "order whatever you like" generosity, never mind that what Collin would like was steak, to his sisters' embarrassment, but a deal's a deal so steak it was.

"Don't go, don't go, please don't go. Can you stay one more night?" Allison begged, but it was time for Becky to catch her plane. "I'll come back," she promised, and when she did she made another IHop run and a splurge at Walmart with a crisp twenty each for Allison ("thank you so much, thank you so much, you're the nicest person in the world") and Collin ("thank you, can I have some more?") both of which equally charmed her.

Yet, Jacquelyn began to notice that Allison, the quietest of the clan, was even quieter still. She never came to Jacquelyn wanting to talk and Jacquelyn did not see her cry much. Some places within the heart of a child are not easily reached.

She'd been watching her little sister from the beginning, and her burden for Allison and her grief process grew, stressed her out, and now weeks into this nebulous life, constantly tugged at her mind. Jacquelyn made a point to ask her how she was feeling and tried to get her sister to tell her her thoughts. Allison remained quiet. Little girls are supposed to be emotional, Jacquelyn thought, not dispassionate.

Jacquelyn would say, "You know, honey, this is hard. How are you feeling about Mommy?"

"I'm sad," Allison would reply and that was it, as closed as a rosebud.

Jacquelyn tried other tactics to get her to confide how she was feeling and what she was going through because she suspected Allison wasn't confiding in anyone and Jacquelyn knew it was unhealthy for a little girl to keep so much pain all to herself. Jacquelyn lay in bed at night thinking up ways to try to get her little sister to talk to her.

"Let's have a cry party," she'd say, which got her nowhere and she felt like she failed. She knew Allison had to have questions and feelings swirling inside her and she didn't want her little sister to be alone in her grief. I want us to be a family that cries together, she thought. That talks about the hard stuff together. But mostly she worried about how this was going to affect Allison, and she was determined not to let her sister, who was old enough to take care of herself physically, but still needed so much, get lost. How can I get her to open up and share her feelings about what's going on? she wondered.

One night, with her father still at the hospital, Jacquelyn tucked Allison in and sat on the edge of her bed in the dark. "Talk time" I had called it—those brief quiet minutes between living the day and falling asleep when I'd flicked off the lights and talked softly to my children, knowing its power as a special entrée into a child's heart, when everything's still, a story's fresh, prayers await, and I listen.

"Honey, it's OK to cry."

Allison lay still, quiet.

"You know," she continued. "This is very sad. What's going on with Mommy is very, very sad. You can cry about it. I know you're sad. And I know you miss her."

Allison nodded, then teared up.

"Jacquelyn?"

"Uh-huh?"

"I'm so afraid of not having a mommy."

Jacquelyn threw her arms around her and held her little sister in the dark, crying with her until the child's tears were spent.

They were still going to be a family. They were going to be the family that rode it out together, with struggles, obviously, but they were going to do it together as a family, she thought, they were not going to be islands.

Claire's challenges were quite different. Up until the moment she had first walked into my ICU room, she had lived in the bliss of her teen world. The night before I'd gone into labor had become a special memory Claire kept pulling out when she needed it, like an old photograph of a loved one taken just before they died that you keep in your pocket until it's frayed at the edges from so much checking. The image says this really happened, this moment in the picture, when they were real and breathing and with me. Claire's snapshot was of that last night when life was normal and she and I had sat and talked. We had talked about her best friend Becky, and boys, about wanting to join the track team at Douglas County High School, about her sister being in college, and most importantly, about the upcoming homecoming dance. "Can I go, Mom?" Claire had asked. "We'll see," I'd said, which was as good as a yes because it wasn't a no, a fact that resurfaced now as she and her dad drove to the hospital, just the two of them, an unusual occurrence in a large family, especially in a large family in crisis.

When Claire was younger she'd read a book about eight-year-old twin girls where the smart twin said to the not-so-smart twin, "It's all about how you play your cards." Driving along with her dad now, fingering the image in the pocket of her mind for its sweet privacy and its embedded fact that she and I had talked about homecoming, she recognized a deal-playing moment.

She was living in that strange place between childhood and adulthood where bits of both edge for dominance, sometimes in the same day, the same hour. Reactions to crisis vary with age and their subsequent developmental ability. Children can sometimes play amidst a crisis while adults stay staggeringly focused, but teens can waver, and that wavering can be mistaken as indifference instead of developing maturity.

"Dad?"

"Uh-huh?" He was her captive audience.

"You know, before all this happened Mom said I could go to homecoming." Not actually a lie, but a truth by default.

"When is it?"

"In about four weeks."

"Who do you want to go with?"

"A big group," which was completely true and the correct card for a winning hand with her father. "Well, a boy from church asked me, but we're going as a group." With his yes Claire relaxed in the passenger's seat and smiled.

Soon after that she went dress shopping with her friend Kirstin and Kirstin's mother and only had intermittent thoughts of how her mother was not the one taking her shopping for her first dance. On the evening of the dance Jacquelyn would drop her off and she would walk a little taller than usual into the house where they were gathering for pictures, as who wouldn't when they're wearing their first grown-up dress, a silver cocktail-length BCBG label with an empire waist, spaghetti straps, and blue beads. They'd take pictures, laugh nervously, get through the pin-the-corsage-on moment. Her date's mom would look at Claire with sad eyes when she'd walk in. "I'm sorry your mom couldn't be here," she'd say. They'd go to Chili's before the dance where they'd pick at chips and salsa and sip Shirley Temples, then pile into cars, laughing, before the music played. But they'd be ready. Claire had seen to that.

One night before the dance and after the dress buying, Claire and Kirstin sat in Kirstin's basement, hanging out, talking and laughing. Mostly laughing. Then Kirstin stopped laughing, looked at Claire with utter solemnity, worry crossing her face.

"Claire," she said. "I don't know how to dance."

Claire looked at her, considered this for a second, then jumped up and began moving to the music streaming from the computer. "You just do this, Kirsti," she said, having only ever danced herself in her bedroom, and the two girls practiced while "Starry Eyed Surprise" played over and over telling them they were going to dance all night, until they were sure that they could.

A home devoid of a mother, and consequently a father who was usually at the hospital, became untenable at night for the younger kids. Allison was the first to ask. "Daddy?" she said one night in the dark. "Daddy, can I sleep in here?" The children had always slept in their own rooms, save for Christmas morning when tradition held that all the kids piled into our king-sized bed to wait for us to wake up enough for everyone to go downstairs together. One night, with Tim at the hospital as usual, Claire climbed into our bed next to Alli who slept soundly. She lay still in my spot, thinking, quiet, and slowly the tide engulfed her. She got back up, remembering that when she'd gone into my closet earlier she'd noticed it smelled like me. She flipped on the closet light, walked in and shut the door behind her, and stood for a moment looking at my shirts, skirts, these familiar fabrics I'd worn, looked at my shoes on the tall shoe rack, and reached out and touched my jewelry. The closet smelled faintly of Obsession, the fragrance I'd worn ever since I'd sent Tim to the perfume counter years ago, telling him "buy something you want to smell on me, my signature scent," and I'd loved it and had worn it on regular days, not just going-out days or dates, because I'd wanted the kids to know my signature scent.

Sure enough, standing here in my closet she smelled "me." She breathed it in and sat down on the closet floor and wept. When is she going to get home? she thought. Is she going to get home? She cried until she'd cried herself to sleep in the still lit closet.

Another night not long after that, in the hours between late night and specks of morning, Claire was in my bed lying next to Allison who slept soundly. The door to my study which was adjacent to our bedroom was closed and the bedroom was dark except for small shafts of light filtered through the double-sided fireplace between our room and my study. The little bit of light wasn't enough to keep her awake but she could hear Tim working at my desk. Tap, tap, tap, he typed away, working on another email update in the deep of the night. She couldn't see him, but she heard his grief, a quiet sob coming from the study, an uncontrollable, can't breathe, can't stop your body from shaking kind of cry coming from her father. Then another.

She sat up to hear better and sat motionless, silent, listening in the near dark. The noise coming from her father sounded like a "God, let her come back to me, why is this happening" kind of sound, she thought. He's crying for his love. He just wants his love back. Claire cried silently for her father's pain, unfiltered, drifting into her earshot.

She waited, listened without moving, straining to hear if he was going to cry out again, wanting to make sure he was OK. Had Allison heard? Her sister still breathed slow, rhythmic breaths. She can't hear Dad do this, Claire thought, not because she thought it was wrong, but because she didn't want her little sister to have to hear what she'd heard, to experience his pain, because no little kid, no kid, should have to hear her dad mourning her mom.

She listened for another thirty minutes, but didn't hear anything more from the study nor did she make a sound herself. She wouldn't let him know he'd been given away.

Tim sat at my desk with no idea Claire was awake. He composed himself and went back to typing the update. He typed for a moment, then stopped and leaned forward, hunching his shoulders at the sudden twinge in his chest. What was that? He sat up straighter and circled his shoulders trying to work out the pain.

6

LIKE EVERY MORNING of the past two weeks the day began with Tim trying to time his morning visit to catch the doctors during early rounds. On this morning Jacquelyn had joined him and the report was bleak. Sometimes in tragedy a small twig of hope floats by in the chaos stream and the drowning grab it, hold tight, until the point when they are rescued or realize that it's just a twig, never meant to be a life preserver. Somewhere in the beginning of the torrent Jacquelyn had picked up the twig of "two weeks." Two weeks, the doctors had said, or at least Tim and Jacquelyn thought. She remembered them saying, "Your mom's in a coma and her body needs time to stabilize from the trauma, let the illness run its course, but then we think we can bring her out of the coma." Jacquelyn thought that surely by two weeks' time there'd be some change, something would get better, rather like when someone has the flu and they're waiting for the fever to break because you know that even though you're still sick you're on the road to recovery. Tim and Jacquelyn had been waiting for the fever to break. And now, two weeks had come and gone. The fever hadn't broken, not even close, and nothing was better. It was, in fact, quite worse.

Standing in the hallway this morning, listening to her father and the doctors discuss the day's bleak news and lack of the expected, hoped-for turning point, she realized with two weeks past that the game had changed completely. She tossed the twig back into the stream and walked outside alone.

She blinked walking out into the bright morning sun and strode across the parking lot to the short-term parking where she'd left the white Jimmy, the family car that had become her car de facto since her mother's disappearance. She yanked open the car door with more force than needed and slid behind the steering wheel, slamming the door closed, then she was still. Pent-up frustration, partially drained, mingled with the growing wave of what she'd been trying so hard to avoid—hopelessness—and she sat there, staring out the windshield, wavering between conflicting emotions, suspended. Just like her life. And the weather agreed; it was one of those clear transition days of early Colorado autumn, neither warm nor cool, a seasonal limbo echoing her mother's, the very weather suspended, like their family.

It's so unfair. So utterly unfair. Jacquelyn grabbed the steering wheel with both hands and sat staring out the windshield at the leaves on the tree in the parking lot median in front of her. She's just another body. Why don't they care that it's been two weeks and she's not getting better? What do I do next? What's next? She stared at the green shimmer of leaves nodding in the breeze, just beginning to turn yellow, looking without seeing, alone in her thoughts.

The two weeks is over. Oh God. I am going to live the rest of my life without my mother. She remembered her grandmother's death when she was nine years old, remembered the pain of losing that woman she was so close to, and knew how much greater this loss was going to be. How can I live life without my mother?

She didn't cry though. Not then. They'd been crying a lot. Instead she sat grim faced, slightly seething, mostly weary, emotionally raw yet numb. She imagined this internal pain without emotional release might be something like what a prisoner of wartime labor camp victim might feel after a long time, when the novelty of pain fades but the situation is unchanged and tears are no longer productive or necessary.

Why isn't God doing anything? Why, with all the prayers, isn't God doing anything? As ICU waiting room veterans they'd seen lots of people in trauma come and go, lots of heartbreaking scenarios, including people who didn't appear to have a faith. And until now, she was like so many American teenagers with a life devoid of real hardship, where all that existed was pleasantness and any unpleasantness had an end cap that would soon relieve her and restore the balance to its rightful sunny ways. Oh in two weeks she'll be better, she thought, mocking her belief in those words. She'd put all her emotional chips on that and it was culminating in a spiritual breakdown, except it wasn't a breakdown because she hadn't been up since it started.

God, why are you doing this to me? I've been a good kid in youth group, I've tried to learn more about you. I thought I was different from those other families in the waiting room that don't know you, but I don't see anything different. If I believe in you, why aren't you helping me out when I need you?

From the most naïve believer to the sagest saint, moments sometimes arise of fleeting (or lingering) spiritual doubt, moments when both ends of the spiritual spectrum and most folks in between admit to thoughts of searing honesty, when they form some shape of an idea that goes like this: I've been a good Christian; now it's time for God to pay me back. Except the idea is usually a subtle, oblique thought, nothing so brazen or straightforward in its near blasphemous tenor, yet the flavor, saint to sinner, can be found in our darkest moments once or twice or more in a life when we are willing to scale away all pretense and admit to the many forms this doubt and questioning can take. And this is the frightening shaky ground Jacquelyn found herself on this morning in the car. She wanted more than anything for God to be like the mafia: you toe the line and God takes care of you.

Except you're not doing that, God! she thought.

This is a sham. This is a farce. Faith is a crutch, a construct to get people through hard times. I have faith, but it's not helping me.

This is all just crap.

And in that moment she began to think, Forget God.

Unbelief tempted with its scent of what it might be like to forget about God, its taste on her lips of denouncing the one she'd aligned with and believed to love, but before she stepped into agnosticism, she let herself wonder what that life would look like without faith in God. And that's when she saw the proverbial fork in the road, in the shape of, well, a fork in the road. In her mind she literally saw a dirt trail with hills in the distance and the trail forked into two distinct paths. Down one path was her life if she chose to abandon faith and abandon God. The other path was her life with God. And she realized, both paths had pain regardless.

She played in her mind what her current life scenario might look like on both paths—crisis with God, crisis without, with an outcome at the end of each. And from her life at that moment in its seeming hopelessness she saw nothing different on either path.

Then another twig floated by.

But hold on. Don't throw away everything you believe and everything you think you believe. Lord, as hard as this is with you, I don't want to do it without you. If I'm already hopeless, I'm going to choose to believe. I'd rather have something than nothing. Life is pain, life is hard, God isn't going to protect you from the reality of the world, but at least, with God, there's hope.

She finished the conversation in her head and got out of the car.

OK great. That was a good decision.

She walked across the parking lot, her long ponytail pulled through the back of her green ball cap, a hint of her mere eighteen years, then she headed back into the hospital to face the next onslaught.

Great. Here come more waves of crap. Great. But . . . I believe in God.

That first week of my coma, Tim took my hand and leaned over me, "Hey, honey," he said softly. "I'm here," but my eyes didn't move under closed eyelids, my body motionless. "I'm here. What a week we're having, aren't we?"

One day he walked into my room with a folded-up page of the *Rocky Mountain News* stuck in his pocket. He was going to read to me. Thoughts of the CT scan incident were pushed aside as he pulled up a chair. "Good afternoon, me pretty," he said. "Why, you ask, am I talking like this? Because Dave Barry said to. I brought you your Dave Barry, hon, you ready?" He scooted a chair up to my bed and sat down, pulled the newspaper page out of his pocket, and unfolded the humor column we'd often read aloud to each other over the years. If he'd gotten to the column first and laughed while he read it, I made him read it to me. If I'd read it first and laughed to myself, I stopped and read it to him, whether he asked for it or not. But he usually did.

Whoosh. Whoosh. Whoosh. "OK, hon, listen up. This one's called 'Arrr talk like a pirate —or prepare to be boarded, by Dave Barry, Sept 8, 2002. Every now and then, some visionary individuals come along with a concept that is so original and so revolutionary that your immediate reaction is: "Those individuals should be on medication."'"

He smiled and looked at me over the page. "You could tell them something about that, huh? Anyway, 'these two guys come up with this idea, Why not have a day when EVERYBODY talks like a pirate? . . .'" Tim finished reading the column, folded it up, and stuck it back in his pocket. If I could have I'd have laughed and told him to read another one and I'd have read one to him and he would have laughed, like always, but the absence of laughter permeated the room.

Tim's chest pains became more frequent. One night during his long drive home from the hospital, his think time, he realized it was entirely possible that he might just keel over, die of a heart attack. What would happen to the children?

However much he tried to hide his fears from them there was no hiding the physical toll. At one stretch Tim had not come home from the hospital for days, was unshowered, unshaven, wearing sleep deprivation like a Halloween mask and he was pallid, pasty with deep sunken eyes. He'd become very, very thin, a haggard ghost of a man wandering around in a battered body.

Jacquelyn left plate after plate of food wrapped up waiting for him when he came home late and plate after plate remained wrapped up the following mornings. When he came home while she was still up he would set his things down on the kitchen table, shuffle through the mail, and she'd nuke the plate she'd saved and set it in front of him.

"Here, Dad, you need to eat."

"Oh thanks, honey. I'm not hungry."

"Dad. You need to eat. You haven't eaten anything today," she'd say, often having witnessed that fact herself. "You look terrible. Dad, you're the only parent we've got," and she tried to hide her fear of walking into our bedroom some morning and finding him halfway between the bed and the bathroom, cold on the floor, dropped dead in an instant in his forties like his father before him. Those were the days she'd quietly pick up the plate and wrap up the food for another meal she knew he'd refuse.

Tim's chest had begun to hurt when he breathed. On a late September night driving home from the hospital he dialed my stepsister Donna's number. She was in her basement doing laundry.

"Donna? It's Tim." His voice came through strained, despondent.

"Hi, Tim."

"I need to ask you something." He choked up. "If Lindsey doesn't make it, and I die, would you and Greg be the guardians of our children if Susan can't?"

"Yes. Of course," and emotion choked her.

He hung up and drove the rest of the way home. He walked

downstairs and opened his metal file cabinet and pulled out the one labeled "Will." He carried it upstairs to my desk, opened his laptop, and began to type.

Addendum to My Last Will and Testament,

I, Timothy P. O'Connor, do hereby amend my Last Will and Testament as follows:

At present the health and continued life of my wife is in doubt. She has suffered complications following the delivery and birth of our 5th child, Caroline Aileen O'Connor. Her present condition is gravely critical, and she may either die or recover with faculties well below that of a functioning adult.

He tackled the latter issue first. If he died but I survived without my faculties a guardian would be needed for the children and me. He appointed my dad, then turned to assigning replacement parents. Our previous will had named Susan, the person most like me. If Susan couldn't do this he appointed Donna and Greg, next in line was my dad, and a fourth fallback was for my father to choose the guardian. Two hours later he finished, a dictum saying I pick you, and you, and you, and you, because my children will not be abandoned, even if the worst happens, because sometimes, it does.

If only they could have just stopped the drugs that kept me comatose and woken me up. It's not that they didn't try—drug vacations they called them—but every time they did, my vital signs dropped. They had to give my lungs time to heal while trying to bring me out of the coma as soon as safely possible, a balance as delicate as a flower.

The pulmonologist called Tim one afternoon with news that he'd had to increase the oxygen setting on the ventilator and they'd discovered blood clots and staph infection in the lungs

51

and blood. Paralytic drugs had been added to immobilize me so the ventilator did all the work, a common occurrence in ARDS patients, paralyzing even the breathing response.

"OK, thanks for telling me," Tim said. About an hour later he got another call, this time from an ICU nurse.

"Tim, Lindsey's oxygen levels are dropping, it's getting worse. I don't know if you understand, but let me explain this to you. They did move her oxygen levels as the doctor told you when he called earlier, but they moved it to 100 percent. What you need to understand is there's no higher setting than that. If this doesn't work and she requires more oxygen, there's nothing more they can do."

He immediately jumped in his car and called my dad.

"I'm headed to the hospital, Pop. I'll meet you guys there."

They sat in stiff blue chairs next to a tall potted palm in the main floor lobby and waited for the few minutes before visiting hours, somber, quiet. He sensed it was time to gather the family.

Tim looked at his father-in-law and leaned closer.

"Pop? Did you bring a suit?"

Crisis to tedium, crisis to tedium to crisis, and again and again; that is life in ICU, and like most families with a loved one critically ill, a crisis routine develops. First thing in the morning Tim called the hospital to get the statistics. Pulse-ox, hematocrit, white count, arterial blood gas. He'd write down the numbers then go back to work, sometimes see me at lunch, return to work until five or five thirty then back to the hospital again before heading home to see our kids.

One thing doctors can provide that patients and patient advocates sometimes lack is the broad view, healing seen as a continuum rather than a minute-by-minute focus on statistics. But that's all Tim had, the metrics he'd learned to read from verbal reports and monitors and conversations with doctors and nurses and drug encyclopedias and research and days on end in the ICU. Fighting tsunamis, treading still water.

Jacquelyn fell into the gravitational pull of the daily statistics too. She began to feel numb, like she couldn't move forward or back because the days just kept repeating themselves. She lived, like Tim, at the mercy of a small paragraph of numbers.

In this suspension Jacquelyn began to think, I wish she would just die. And then guilt would overpower her that she'd actually formed that thought. Then she reasoned with the guilt: I can't continue to live every day stuck on the numbers, the status quo unmoving, a mother who wasn't living and wasn't dead. It's killing me, killing Dad, all of us. Then she'd turn: I will see her again, I don't grieve like those who have no hope.

She wondered if this must be how the parent of a kidnapped child feels, who never recovers a body, a lost loved one never found, and the wound in their being and life can't close. A grief suspended. I wasn't cold in the grave so she couldn't grieve like I was. I was the undead, alive but not living, missing, lost.

They were suspended above, I was suspended in the deep, in the belly of the whale, which Aldous Huxley called something peculiarly horrible, a visceral prison. It was also what George Orwell wrote in his essay "Inside the Whale": "The whale's belly is simply a womb big enough for an adult. There you are, in the dark, cushioned space that exactly fits you, with yards of blubber between yourself and reality, able to keep up an attitude of the completest indifference, no matter what happens . . . Short of being dead, it is the final, unsurpassable stage . . ." Surely, in some deep level of my subconscious I screamed, Get out of the bed! Leave the whale! Embrace my baby, protect her.

A visceral prison, a womb in the middle seas, just short of that terminable end, but just short; I was Jonah caught, waiting to be spit out.

7

TIME HAD BECOME IRRELEVANT. It held me, rocked me, trapped me, and freed me. I couldn't come or go and was unbound from the cues and awareness of the passing of time. No calendars, no Tuesday, no 1:00, no dawn or dusk, no waking with sun or sleeping by moon. There was no past or future, two places we humans spend so much mind time. I had only one place to be and I was always there.

Where was I in the sea of unconsciousness? Comatose? Semicomatose? Semiconscious? In an altered state of consciousness? Preconscious? What do those things even mean? Precise definitions are tough to nail down because patients' experiences of the different states of consciousness are individual, and this area of science is in ongoing research, still shrouded in mystery. The basic meaning of consciousness, though, is an awareness of one's environment and one's own existence, thoughts, the life of the mind, but levels of consciousness are a fluid continuum, less like a light switch, more like a preheating oven.

The most common measuring stick of sorts doctors use to assess a patient's level of consciousness rather than ambiguous definitions and subjective labels is the Glasgow Coma Scale—an evaluation that measures responses to external stimuli in three areas: eye response, ability to respond with speech or sounds, and response with movement. It's scaled from 3 to 15 (with

3 being the lowest possible score and where I spent so much time); a score below 9 is a coma, between 9 and 11 is partially conscious, and 15 is fully aware.

The lowest end of this scale is coma—deep unconsciousness from which a person cannot be aroused, with a complete absence of response to stimuli—no eye opening, verbal or motor response, no voluntary movement, no response to pain, noise, or light, no sleep-wake cycle. A person in a vegetative state may respond reflexively to some stimuli, such as flinching away from pain, but they are not aware of the world around them. When a person stays at this level for a prolonged period, usually three months or more, it's considered a persistent vegetative state. In a minimally conscious state the patient has intermittent awareness and wakefulness, sometimes able to interact with the world in a limited way. They may follow simple verbal commands, make purposeful movements, may have intelligent verbalizations.

A person waking from a coma may spend only a few days working their way up the scale and back to full awareness, but many times it's an agonizing process of widely varying chunks of time with no guarantee that once they begin to wake up, they will recover fully; some people get stuck at one level for the rest of their lives and never return to full consciousness. Others, even with drug-induced comas, return to consciousness at widely varying rates, and some sustain cognitive impairments.

Waking from a coma, moving through the levels of consciousness into full awareness, is complex, different for each patient, and isn't at all like it's depicted in most movies. It's no *While You Were Sleeping*, the 1995 Sandra Bullock movie. Not at all. In fact, one 2006 Mayo clinic medical study found that almost all movie depictions of awakenings after coma are inaccurate. They get the family's experience and the neurologist depiction wrong, and the patients are often caricatures—well-groomed, tanned, muscular "Sleeping Beauties" without feeding tubes, tracheostomy, muscle wasting, and other realities.

Miraculous awakenings with a lack of cognitive deficits or any long-term effects where the patient suddenly opens their eyes and starts speaking as though nothing ever happened, and stays fully awake and aware, are not reality. And here's the thing—not only did many of the nonmedical viewers in the study think the depictions were accurate, almost 40 percent said they thought if a loved one were in a coma the movies would influence their real-life decisions. However, one movie that captured a more realistic sense of what a family sees and experiences when a loved one is comatose is the 2011 award-winning movie *The Descendants* starring George Clooney. When my family watched it years after our experience we were deeply moved.

Years after my illness a scene in another movie resonated and shook me viscerally at what seemed like some cellular level of recognition when I watched Julian Schnabel's 2008 film adaptation of Jean-Dominique Bauby's book *The Diving Bell and the Butterfly*. Bauby had been the French editor of *Elle* magazine and in 1995, at age forty-three, he suffered a stroke paralyzing his entire body except for his left eye. He eventually learned to communicate by blinking through the alphabet and blinked out his beautiful memoir. He emerged from a coma to experience Locked-In Syndrome, cognizant and lucid while trapped in a body that cannot move. The film captured Bauby's awakening scene as if the audience were looking through his eyes, rising from a place of darkness until gauzy light comes into focus, then people, with whom he can see and hear but not communicate. I did not have Locked-In Syndrome, but I watched Schnabel's version of Bauby's coma awakening and shuddered with flashes of recognition of what it was like to move through and emerge from layers of consciousness, and I wept with the remembering.

In the latter stages of the coma the me inside the life-supported body drifted through the levels of awareness and caught specks of reality, snatches of conversation, and merged them with my subconscious and the life of my mind. Thoughts within and happenings around me would meet, swirl and dip, form, then recede, float past each other, slide through each other like colliding tendrils of smoke.

This is one of those moments.

". . . you're in ICU . . . Swedish Hospital . . . honey? . . ."
I am so tired. I open my eyes, Tim is there. I close my eyes,
sleep. Open them again, no one's there. Then a nurse. She doesn't
seem to look at me. So tired. Must sleep . . .

I think I'm lost. I am definitely somewhere, but where? Tim
seems to keep finding me so I can't be very lost; it's such a good
thing he's so smart, he keeps finding me. He is sometimes sitting beside me when I wake up and sometimes I work hard to
keep my eyes open, straining to hear him rounding the corner,
waiting, then he walks in and relief washes over me; I am safe
again, found again. And I close my eyes . . .

The room is dark now. Silver rails, narrow rods with a groove
in the middle line the ceiling above me, encircling the area I'm
lying in. Another rail outlines a similar space next to mine,
and another, making a metal grid across the ceiling. It's dark
in here, pitch, in fact, the cold causing the darkness. I'm in a
boxy space outlined by the metal. I notice there's a box for a
person above me, below me, to the left, to the right, like Hol-
lywood Squares and spaces for people next to them comprising
a big three-dimensional grid and I am in the middle. We are all
floating. In the dark. In the cold. There are other people in their
grids, sometimes, then they're gone and it's just me, hovering
in my space, a space I know I am absolutely not to leave. Then
I hear her coming. I try to hide, want to pull a curtain around
me, but she finds me and I try to smile.

She's wearing white and a mocking smile that stares through
me, lips turned up at the corners only, eyes cold, filling the room
with cold, eyes squinty enough to make you think she's smiling, but they leak out the truth from the middle, spilling out
disdain, bits of malice.

"Lindsey?" She calls out my name from a distance and I look
around trying to find the disembodied voice.

I want to answer her. She has so many things I need although I'm not sure what they are but she's going to help me

out of here. I want to trust her. I need to trust her. I want out of this place.

She calls my name again, and her voice is closer this time. I have to help her find me so she can help get me out of here because this place is dangerous. I try to answer her, but my voice falls off into the dark, like feathers off a cliff. I need to find her, need her to find me.

"You're going to be just fine," she calls down to me while she works with someone else. She walks quickly to me, looks me over with her cold, smirking eyes.

"What do you need?" she asks. "You're fine." I step back.

She turns and walks away, peering over her shoulder at me, disappears into another black floating cubicle with another body. I want to hide in the corner and whisper in the dark to them, "What do you think of this place? What do you think of her? I think we should be careful."

I watch her pull a blue vial out of her pocket, stick the needle in and pull back and flick, flick the syringe. Quickly, deftly, she brings her arm forward and jabs the needle into the person next to me and the person falls into a heap. The woman in white's eyes glint. The lifeless form is removed. All the spaces are empty now except for mine, all dark except for the dim light that enfolds her. She's murdered them all! I realize. Suddenly I know what I have to do.

Run.

She doesn't know I've seen her. I have to get out. Out of this place, but I can't let her know what I have just witnessed, that I know she is not my caretaker but my assailant and my jailer.

She discards the needle, turns and begins walking toward me. My heart races, the cold in the room shoots into my bones as the adrenaline pulses through my body and I look for an escape. Her footsteps get nearer and I try to quiet my breathing. I look up at the rails, around at all the empty spaces, nowhere to run, no place to hide, no way to escape.

Her footfalls stop. She stands next to me, her arm behind her back.

Her ice eyes look at me.

"You're going to be just fine," she hisses.

I wake barely enough to know this wasn't real, but I'm shaken and the feeling of terror lingers. I'm alone in my glass-walled ICU room with metal tracks on the ceiling holding a privacy curtain, and once, maybe twice, I heard an ICU nurse, one who had a problem with Tim, enter my room and say what sounded sardonic to me, "You're going to be just fine."

Years later I will discover that nightmares during comas are a common occurrence and sometimes they merge images and sounds and experiences of what's happening around them with the unbridled stories of a dreaming mind, including nightmares of fear and death and being held captive. I'm so grateful that Tim believed and defended one piece of advice he'd been given: hearing is a sense that can remain after all others are gone. He'd been the sentry enforcing his order for the two months I slept that no one should say anything in my comatose presence that they would not say had I been awake.

I wish I had memories stacked to the sky of the countless lovely things that were said, sung, and prayed then, of the nurses who saved my life with their tender care and words, and sometimes I imagine I remember them all. Yet, what mother doesn't stand over her baby's crib watching her sleep and whisper, "I love you," sing lullabies soft, which we don't expect them to remember, but we know the love soaks in, matters.

Dreams dissolve and I feel the compression boots squeeze my calves then deflate and release again and again, a background refrain. I feel my leg and bladder muscles tensing.

I have to get up. I'll open my eyes and get up. Why aren't I moving? Get up. Walk to the bathroom. Get up!

I hear a nurse come in and walk around the foot of my bed, busy with her job, silent.

Just tell her. I need to go. Say it. Get up. Then in an instant she walks away, out of my room and I'm alone, incapable of pressing the call button even if I were aware of it.

Stay awake. Don't wet the bed. Catch the nurse. Hold it. Stay awake. Stay awake. Don't wet the bed. Catch the nur . . .

I awaken again to the sound of rubber soles padding on linoleum around me. Is it another day? Another week? Bathroom. Bathroom. Did I mouth the word or think it?

"Oh, it's OK," she says, "Just go ahead and go," then she's gone again.

In the bed? She wants me to go in this bed? I close my eyes and wait and wait, trapped in the bed and my thoughts until I think I can hold it no longer.

Another day or hour or moment I need to move my bowels. I hear the nurse in my head, "just go ahead." Why? How can this be OK? I hold it until I feel I might burst from the holding, then suddenly I lay covered in humiliation and shame and bewilderment until I am asleep.

A nurse lifts the sheet. "Oh my goodness," she says and pulls the sheet off of me. "Oh you really did it," she says, disgust in her voice, and begins the long task of cleanup. "Man," she continues to mutter and I realize she is not speaking to me. I can't speak to her. I can't help her, I just submit to being turned and cleaned like a baby, turned again to remove soiled sheets, turned again for new ones to be put on, all done to me and around me like I am a mannequin in the bed. Except for one important difference. I am a mannequin who can hear.

Perhaps she let slip the disgust some nurses no doubt must feel occasionally because it's easier to let the truth slip out when you think no one hears you.

I hear her muttering and complaining while she cleans me of everything but my humiliation and I don't know which is worse, what I've just had to do, or hearing the disgust in her voice for what she had to do. Shame settles on me, heavy.

I sleep again and dream about inappropriate defecation and inappropriate comments.

8

THERE HAVE ONLY BEEN A FEW TIMES in my life when I thought I might die, thought I was precariously close and could slip over the precipice in a shot, but there has only been one moment in my life when I thought I *was* dying, thought I was actually in the act of dying. Some voices or a touch stay with you forever.

The week after my first awakening, my kidneys were failing, another ARDS complication, and I came very close to dying. During the last two weeks of October, doctors had to resume coma-inducing sedation. There were moments in this latter part of my two months of unconsciousness when I could hear, but not respond. Tim picked up my hand and said, "Honey, can you hear me?" I wonder how many times he must have said that. I hear another man talking to Tim, the drone of their voices far away.

"Lin, the doctor's here." I could see nothing but I heard every word. "Hon, the doctor wants to talk to you." OK. The doctor wants to talk to me.

"Lindsey, I'm Dr. . . . " blah, blah blah. I felt both my hands being held, the warmth of their skin, the feel of my thumbs on top of their hands.

"Lindsey," the doctor said, "I need you to squeeze my hand." Pause. "Can you do that for me?" Pause.

"Honey, if you can hear us please squeeze our hands."

Such a simple request.

Squeeze their hands. Squeeze their hands. Just a little.

My mind responds but my body does not.

I can't squeeze their hands. Oh God. I cannot squeeze their hands! Maybe I'm dying.

In that moment I felt lost between two worlds, unable to enter the one I so desperately wanted to be in, hearing, not seeing, unable to force my body to tighten my hand muscles in the slightest way. I was thoughts on the pillow.

Their voices shifted from speaking to me to speaking about me and I notice I'm being spoken of in third person, but who could blame them? They hadn't offended my sensibilities, after all, they'd only wanted me to tighten my grip on their fingers and thumb, even one digit. I desperately wanted to tell them that I heard them, that I understood, that I was trying, trying to do this one little thing and that I could still hear them talking. I wanted them to know that I could not will myself to respond, that I knew I was dying.

I felt death like a soft kiss. I wasn't tortured or sad because sadness is a state of heart, emotion born from the awareness that what you want or love is not what you wish it to be, for example, and I was not aware at that moment that I was a mother. There is a degree of sickness when you forget the strongest, most profound bonds you know. If I had been able to think about my children and realize I might indeed be leaving them motherless, that I even had any children at all, I think sadness would have washed me away. Instead I felt indefinable regret, because regardless of the pain and suffering and otherworldliness I lay in, I did not want to die. I had been in a coma for two months, could not breathe or eat or move unassisted, could not communicate, but . . . I longed to live. I was—and remain—awed at the staggering sheer force of the will to live.

I felt a calm, unemotional sense that my existence was connected by a thin thread, invisible, immaterial, to my life and the one I believe begins when this one ends. A thin, unsentimental, quiet thread.

I am sitting up in a chair. I hear faint noise I can't quite make out, a constant hum of voices and life going on and things unidentifiable. I sense someone has come into the room. They are on my left. They walk past me, pause, walk around the foot of the empty bed to the other side of the room and I have a sense of watching them walk by in my peripheral vision. I hear them speak and it's different from the distant droning noise I've heard. I want more of it. I don't know who it is, cannot see them clearly, it's as if I'm looking and listening through inch-thick opaque glass, underwater. We are in the same space, but separated. I want to join them, to talk.

I'm here. I'm over here. Do you know that? Do you know that I'm talking to you? Are we having a conversation? I can't tell. No, I don't think we are. I only wish. But if I keep talking to you like this and you don't leave and I keep hearing your voice, it's OK. It'll be OK.

Then I realize there's no point in making an effort to reach them because they are unreachable. They can't hear me. So for now I'm left with a peculiar fusion of longing for the warmth of connecting that I cannot make and resignation that I am here and they are there and that's just the way it is. Separated, but together, me and someone, a chair, distant noise, warm noise, longing, time and more time. What would I have thought at the time if I had known I was strapped into a chair with the television turned on to "stimulate me"?

When we have a physical need we can be completely focused on meeting that need. If I need a Motrin or a drink of water or a bathroom now, don't expect me to be able to listen to you talk about your grandmother or your cat unless your grandmother is bringing me a Motrin and a drink and your cat is showing me to your bathroom. I have no idea what I needed that day in the second hospital's intensive care unit, but I remember that getting that need met became my sole focus and I was powerless to do anything about it myself.

With the very sick it often takes a team to save a life—doctors in multiple disciplines, a patient advocate (a trusted person acting as the patient's voice on their behalf and communicating between the patient and providers, which I believe every hospitalized person needs), and nurses (the front-line daily caregivers). Tim was my patient advocate; I had topnotch doctors in pulmonology, neurology, cardiology, critical care, multi-trauma, infectious disease, nephrology, and radiology (whew); and excellent ICU staff (whom I think should have pro-football player paychecks). But sometimes, in a sea of awesome it's the troubling moments that stay with us. It was very late in October, some two months after this had begun, during some of the latter stages of the coma, perhaps a moment somewhere in the minimally conscious state, an intermittent period one afternoon when I was briefly and vaguely aware of my surroundings. I could hear and see things close around me in my ICU bed, and remembered the concept of hours on a clock. Tim was coming soon. And I needed . . . something. A drink? To be moved because of pain? More likely. A call button is designed for the sick, even the very sick, to be able to press a tiny little button without much effort and summon help. I remember looking at it, wishing I could make it do its job. Wishing a nurse would whoosh in, get into my field of vision with a smile, pat my arm and say, How are you? Is there anything I can do for you? And I'd nod and mouth the words pain, hurt, tubes, and she or he would immediately know that there was an ax lodged in my side and they must remove it immediately. Reach for the button. You can do it. Press it. They'll come. But I can't. And they aren't. Lie there needing, needing. Drift off. Sleep. Wake up. Needing. Inching for help. But help is still just out of reach.

". . . birthday . . . come on in here . . . ," I hear someone say beyond my room.

There is laughter offstage, in that pool of dark. The smell of popcorn drifts into my room.

"cake . . . get a piece . . ." Laughter. More voices now. More laughter.

Drift off. Wake up. Then I got an idea.

I saw a spoon on the bedside table. I reached for it, grabbed it and with limited movement tapped the spoon against the table. The staff was right outside my door. They were having a party. Just a tiny one I'm sure. I'll bang this spoon, get their attention, then they'll put down that cake, stop eating that popcorn, and swoop in here saying, Oh we're sorry, so and so turned forty today or is leaving for Zimbabwe and we were celebrating but, honey, we're watching your every move, monitoring all this stuff you're hooked up to and you're just fine. Just fine. But what can I do for you? I heard you bang that spoon. Can't you reach your call button? Oh you can, but you can't press it? I'd nod. She'd take the spoon, pat my arm, shift my body, and the ax would fade away.

I banged again. Waited. And again. A small flick of my wrist of metal on hard plastic created a small noise but a noise I was certain they could hear, those people I listened to right outside my room. Bang. Wait. Listen. Bang. Bang. Listen. Bang, bang, bang, bang. Tap, tap, tap, tap.

Laughter.

Bang, softer now, drifting off again.

Then he's there. I open my eyes, see Tim. I am once again rescued.

"They wouldn't come," I mouth. "I banged for two hours, but they wouldn't come." "Two hours?" A look came over his face that I understood to mean that he knew exactly what I'd said, what I needed, and what had just transpired. His jaw tightened and all the anger and frustration I'd felt for the past two hours flowed right off me onto him, and he absorbed it, embraced it, picked it up on his broad shoulders with ease and immediacy. My body relaxed.

"You understand me," I mouthed. I knew it wasn't easy for others to read my lips and understand my effort to communicate, but perhaps his ability had less to do with him being my husband and knowing me and more to do with his effort, his bending down close, watching my mouth intently. And simply being there. Just being there.

"I'll be back," he said, his quick, heavy footsteps leaving.

I had lain there needing what I could not do for myself and without relief of that need for hours, without an answer to my call for help, not because they couldn't hear me. It wasn't the cake, the popcorn, the laughter, or the guy going to Zimbabwe keeping them from coming into my room. They'd heard my spoon banging. The whole time. One common characteristic of a person with brain damage is repetitive motion. Motion without meaning, without thought or purpose, an uncontrollable repetition of a particular response, a tick of one whose mind is not working properly. It's called perseveration. Someone perseverating can repeatedly flail their arms or, say, bang a spoon, because they are brain damaged. This is what those on duty that day assumed about me. I lay brain damaged and didn't warrant a response.

I'm just going to get up for a minute, I think. Reach up, grab the rail, stretch my legs, and I'll be right back in the bed. I'll just be a second.

"Dear, lay back. Just relax. You can't do that," a nurse says, sweet and calm.

Whatever.

"Relax. Just relax." She pats my arm and makes some movement to stop me from trying to sit up, but I don't want to relax. I want to get up a sec, then come right back and go back to sleep. I try to get up again. My legs are so heavy. Why are my legs so heavy? I have to kick these covers off.

Then Tim breezes in and he's standing now at the foot of my bed.

"Whoa, honey, what are you doing?" he asks, putting his hands on my legs, "Where you going?" He smiles, appears a little bit amused and now I'm getting ticked. I just want to get up. What's the matter with you people?

"Hon, you're not going anywhere." He makes me lie down again and chuckles.

What is wrong with them? Why is he laughing? I want to hit him. I make the meanest face I can, crinkle my eyebrows in the fiercest way, give him that look, that I-am-so-not-happy-with-you look, but he laughs again, with odd, tender amusement.

They won't let me get up and they're laughing. This is so rude.

What I know now was that day I didn't know that I couldn't. My brain, picking back up from my last moments of conscious, when I had walked into the hospital, believed I could.

9

I HAVE AN IDEA," Tim says, "I'm going to run to my car. I'll be right back." A few moments later he walks in with his computer. "Let's try this," he says. He plugs it in and stretches the cords out and carries it toward me, holds it perched over the railing of my bed, his eyes eager. I can just type to communicate he tells me. He'll talk, I'll type.

"Do you want to try this?" he asks, his voice filled with hope and anticipation.

Yes. This is a great idea. My fingers fly on a keyboard. Sure I'll try. I nod. He raises the back of my bed and carefully moves the tubing around me out of the way. Slowly he puts a pillow on my lap, and places the laptop on the pillow. I look up at Tim and for the moment he is all that matters, looming large like a movie close-up. I look down at the computer in front of me now, the tool of my writing life, as comfortable and familiar to me as an oar to a sculler.

I put my hands on the smooth black surface and he moves it again aligning the computer to the angle of my arms, adjusting the machine into typing position with my body instead of the norm where one adjusts one's body into typing position over the machine. I perch my hands over the keyboard; I haven't needed to move in the bed. I don't know yet, however, that significant movement in the bed is not possible now.

My fingers bend and hover millimeters above the keys, instinctively close to home row but off. He inches the computer to one side a bit. "Is that better?" he asks. I move my fingers slightly one set of keys over. I rest them on the keys.

"That's it," he says, and he waits, eager to read what's going on in my head, to communicate in a way that's natural for me. I have no idea yet how hungry he is for me to talk to him, how for almost two months he has talked to me, his silent, lost, nonresponsive wife. He has told me he loves me, what the weather is for the day, where the children are that day, that I'm going to get better, that it's going to be OK, that I'm being taken care of, that I wouldn't believe who all has come to visit and how so many people are helping him, and that he wants me to wake up. For forty-seven days he's talked to me; a one-sided conversation with a shell of a woman who was with him one minute and gone the next, who'd talked to him for some two decades but the past some two months only answered him with slight rises in heartbeats at the sound of his voice, eyes closed, body still, voice gone. And now finally, I can answer him, mutely, through my voice on the page. He leans over the bed peering onto the screen, supports my back with his arm.

I touch the keys, but my fingers don't move.

I lift my fingers slightly. Touch them down again to the keys. Rest them there. He waits and doesn't say anything.

I think about this. I should reach my fingers out and to the side and move them over the keys; there's a rhythm, a pace, a way to move my fingers and strike the letters, from the keys to the screen creating words, sentences, books, but now, my fingers don't reach out or up, they don't press down into that automatic groove of hands and keyboard. They just rest on the keys, fingers curled. Still.

I concentrate. He wants me to do this. This is important to him. It's a good idea. Let's see . . .

My fingers don't move.

"You OK, honey?" he asks. I nod, fingers poised. Fingers still. Seconds pass. Long, still seconds. A minute passes and another. I sense that nurses are busying themselves with things in my room around me, coming in and going out, but are watching me. Will the silent woman "speak"?

But I do not. I do not move my fingers to make the words my husband longs to hear on the page.

"That's OK, honey," he says. "You're tired. It's OK. We can try this again later," and he slides the computer out from under my still fingers. "You just rest now," he says. I look up at him, catch his eye as he lifts the computer over the hospital rail, unplugs it, replaces it in its case.

Yes, I'm tired, I think. Thank you. I'm so glad you know I'm tired, that I can't think. Can't think. Can't think to type. Can't type. I look at him and am relieved he says no more. I watch him put it all away and I wonder and am so very grateful and a little stunned. I couldn't type. Why? Yes, I'm tired like he said. I look at him, he smiles softly, and then we both sort of wonder, but also know.

I do not remember how to type.

There's still so much I'm unclear about even now, years later, so much I'll never know, like layers and layers of baby Swiss cheese, holes lapping over substance, but when peeled apart, you still find holes. I keep doing what any good reporter trying to keep at a story does—as new questions in an old story surface, go back to your primary source. So much later I do.

"Tim, remember the day you first brought Caroline to me after I woke up?" I've called him at work because I'm trying to remember this and I'm unclear when exactly it happened. It's a memory floating, without context, and I need him to ground it for me. "She was wearing a red outfit. Sharon handed her to me. What day was that? Was it October 15th?"

"Well, there were two days. Which one do you mean?"

"Two days?"

"Can we talk about this tonight?"

"Sure, but you remember?"

"Yeah, but I don't have time right now to explain it."

I hang up feeling a little like when you get to the end of a chapter in the book you're reading and you get one question answered only to have another question raised, so you turn one more page because you really want to know what happens, except you have to stop reading now because it's time to fix dinner or the house is on fire or something and you're a little irritated because this unanswered question's still hanging out there and you want to read a little longer but you can't. I have a single memory of waking from unconsciousness and being presented with my baby. And now there are two days, another page to turn, another layer of Swiss to peel back.

Tim leans over the metal bed rail, drapes his long torso over it so his face is so close to mine I can feel his breath. It's what he does now when he comes into my room. Comes straight to me, kisses me, but then instead of pulling back into the normal spatial distance of daily domestic life—like say a couple has when they're standing in the kitchen sipping the last of their coffee before leaving for work, or sitting next to each other watching TV—he stays close. He turns and checks my oxygen saturation and heart rate, then hones back to that close place, his new custom. I didn't think about it at the time, but it drew me from the deep, tethered me to consciousness.

He'd told me my friend Sharon was bringing the baby to see me. I think he asked if I wanted to see her, if I was ready. Sure, I nodded. Why not.

Sharon walked in carrying the baby in her arms and stood next to me doing the mother-sway, smiling the whole time, telling me about how alert and contented the baby was. She held her out to me like a presentation of a bottle of fine wine. She was wearing red knit pants with a white top and red jacket, and little baby shoes. Her top was tucked in. She looked . . . big to me. Fat. I didn't have fat babies. Not that I would have minded a fat baby, I'd just never had one.

I looked at her and the baby and tried to take it all in. I don't remember what Tim did except that he seemed torn between sharing Sharon's pride in his beautiful baby and excitement in this moment, and his tending to me, moving, adjusting my paraphernalia. In that close place he said, "Honey, are you ready to hold her?" I nodded.

They laid the baby on my lap, supporting her for me. It seemed like Sharon was especially focused on making the introduction of me and this child and Tim seemed preoccupied with keeping my tubes away from tiny fists. I looked down at her.

Red clothes. Pink skin. Wide-open eyes. Fat. She wasn't crying. I thought she looked like a nice baby. I'd had this baby before everything went dark. I'd lived, she'd lived, and now here we were together, finally, which is what had everyone in the room (who all I can't remember) so excited. Their exuberance level seemed at a 10 and mine was a 1, maybe a 1.5, but since my body was still on life support, my voice inaccessible, there was no pressure to move or speak to try to reach their mood, even though I knew in some deep place that they'd probably appreciate a little more from me. But I couldn't do anything about it. It simply was what it was and no more, nothing close to what you imagine a moment like this should be. From my vantage point it was an unembellished moment, this baby in red, lying in front of me. At some point near the end of the visit I looked down and thought, this is that baby. I'm so glad she lived. She seems like such a nice baby. Really big, but nice.

Sharon and Tim told me all about her and I lay there, still, and listened. I understood—this was my baby—but . . . I wonder when her mother's going to come get her.

Many months later when I'm home and Tim has handed me the pack of "not so bad" pictures, I look for the first time at the single shot of this day, "Red Outfit Day" as I've thought of it, and even that mental identifier I've given it is telling since you'd think I would have called it "Meet My Baby Day" or "First Time Ever I Saw Her Face Day" or something. The image is a contrast of joy and bleakness. I see a not particularly plump baby in red, lying on my lap, ventilator tube trailing above her head, Tim, smiling, holds her head and shoulders while Sharon, smiling, feeds her a bottle. I am looking down at her, almost expressionless, the baby's eyes not meeting mine. And then, looking at this picture, I see it. My hands rest on the bed, not the baby. My infant had been placed in my lap for the first time of which I am aware since those first five minutes two months ago, and I was not even attempting to touch her. The first time I saw this, all doubt fell away that my lack of bonding might be in any way a mirage, and I cried.

10

My snippets of memory had no grounding in the continuum of time, no sense of where those moments fit, unlike life lived fully conscious where we live chronologically—this happened before, this is happening now, this is what may happen tomorrow—and we can think of it visually because of the tools we use to wrangle meaning and order out of our minutes. Timers, clocks, watches, calendars, Day-timers, tools absent from my life for over two months. I've had to order my memories of my 107 days and beyond even, from the chronology of my family and friends' lives. "When did that happen? Did this happen before that? What day was that? Which came first?" Even, "what month was that?" I've had to piece together aural, visual, sensory snapshots like a giant jigsaw puzzle and become content that there will always be big sections of the puzzle that are lost forever. Yesterday while vacuuming the dining room I found a tiny piece of blue cardboard, dropped from the 1000-piece puzzle a few weeks earlier. I reached down and picked up the piece, brushed the dust off it, and stuck it in my pocket to put it away later. I continue to occasionally find little pieces of the whole picture that I dust off, stick in my pocket, ask for help finding where the piece goes from others who know what the picture looks like.

November 6, 2002, was a watershed day for me. For the first time since August 30th, I was lodged into a sentient state where I stayed, finally. Except no one knew it but me. I'd been moved out of ICU into a room on the fourth floor, MTU, the multi-trauma unit, which sounds bad but is way better than ICU. I have no memory of being moved out of ICU or any specific moments of waking up in room 4273. On this day I notice the calendar hanging on the wall opposite me. I focus, find the square on the calendar with the same 6 that the nurse had written on the whiteboard that day along with her name. What happened on the squares to the left of the 6 I have no idea, but there I am, on that square, and the square to the right, the 7, would be tomorrow.

It would still be another week or two before it struck me that I'd also been plucked into an entirely different season. I'd gone to sleep at the end of summer; I awoke in autumn. On November 6th, Calendar Day I've always called it, my awareness shifts, my mind grasps again the abstract concept of time, puts me in context, where minutes start lining up, stay in order, play nice; it's the first day that time begins to line up and march in step, proper-like, and I begin to live and perceive chronologically again.

Sharing life events and emotions we experience with those to whom we're closest is a profound human need. Who doesn't remember who they called on 9/11 or who we'd tell if we get a parking ticket? We go through stuff, we talk about it with the ones we love—human connection hardwiring. Now that I was awake and aware and apparently staying that way, my family and best friends began the job of telling me, for my benefit and theirs, what had happened the two months I'd been some place other.

Tim, Jacquelyn, Kathy, and Claire, the key storytellers early on, did so with great patience and, I see now, wisdom, fluctuating between my capacity and need to know, and their need to tell, all of which varied daily. I could only handle small bits of information at a time, from a brain-processing perspective as well as an emotional one. They'd see me tire and stop. On bad days they spared me the story, on less bad days I'd learn a little more, and lots of days they'd repeat the parts I'd already forgotten.

The first Sunday after Calendar Day was a reuniting of souls—Tim stayed with me the entire day and I was "present" for it, and it felt a little like a long-anticipated couple's getaway, without the room service bagels and cream cheese and the *Sunday Times*. In a strange verbal role reversal, I, who previously wrote and talked for a living, was voiceless, and he, introverted, man-of-few-words, could finally, after waiting two months, communicate with me. His story of what had happened to me, to him, a single event we shared, but experienced separately, spilled out of him with an urgent intensity I'd never seen—it was the day his verbal dam broke.

"It was the worst thing I'd ever gone through in my life and I couldn't talk to you about it," he says.

I think that's what it's sometimes like when someone you love dies, you need to tell them what you're going through, but you can't. Now we were getting a second chance and so much gratefulness fills the room I think the walls might explode.

"You can't imagine what August 30th was like," he says, shaking his head a little, his face intent, his eyes looking up with the remembering and he begins at the beginning, the point right after my lights went out. "It was like a scene from a movie. Nurses were running, literally running down the hall carrying bags of blood. All together you got twenty units of blood and blood products."

"Wow," I mouth. He lets this sink in. I know what a bag of blood hanging from an IV pole looks like and I imagine twenty of them lined up for me; I'm in near unbelief that this is about twice the amount of blood in my body.

That Sunday Tim sat on the end of my bed reliving the call he got at home from one of the doctors during the first week. "They told me you were very ill," he says, "but the utmost issue to the medical team at this point was their concern over a brain injury as a result of oxygen deprivation from the blood loss the first night. I remember exactly what the doctor said: 'We think there's been a brain injury, but we can't pinpoint the severity of it until after the lungs heal and she's removed from the medications since we can't really diagnose the severity of this type of injury on somebody's who's in a drug-induced coma.'"

He tells me this and I see the pain on his face. I tap my finger to my temple and mouth to him, "What were you thinking?"

"I thought, a brain-damaged wife? Unthinkable! The doctor told me they were bringing in a neurologist to see you and they were going to do some baseline brain scans and expected some degree of injury."

I'm tired from the exertion of listening and processing what he's telling me, but I don't want him to stop talking.

"I brought my computer, honey," he says. "Can I read you some of the email updates I started writing to keep everyone informed?" I nod, eager to hear. He took out his computer, fired it up, and got comfortable on the end of my bed, and as he begins reading I'm transported back two months into his experience, his pain, written at the time it was happening. "This is the first one I wrote," he says and starts reading.

> *Update (#1) on Lindsey from Tim,*
> *All,*
> *First, let me say that words cannot express deeply enough the gratitude, blessing and comfort I and my children have in knowing that so many are praying for us. THANK YOU ALL.*
> *On the medical front, on Friday, the medical staff made two attempts during the day to move Lindsey up to the room for the MRI test they want to do on her brain. In order to do that, it requires that she be disconnected from her vent machine and manually vented for the trip to the MRI room. Both times resulted in a drop in vital signs— primarily oxygenation—so that the nurses were forced to*

cancel the test. (On the second attempt, she made it to just outside the door of the MRI room before they stopped and returned her to ICU.)

The pulmonologist is also pursuing more information that would explain the decline in Lindsey's lung function over the course of the past week.

Last evening, I took Caroline up to be with Lindsey—laid the baby on her chest again. During this time, Lindsey tried to open her eyes—Praise our God!!!! We plan to repeat this "treatment" for Lindsey and Caroline as often as is practical.

God bless you All,
Tim

I cry softly.

"I took a picture of that. I've got a packet of pictures actually at home. Do you want to see them?" he asks. I nod and he tells me he will bring them soon, then he reads update number two, and three, stopping when his voice cracks from the remembering, gathering his composure, then reading the next one. He reads to me, inserting backstory commentary along the way, for hours, and finally, we are doing what people who love each other are supposed to do: share and bear each other's pain.

He is able to lip-read what I say, with a few retries at times, better than anyone.

"Did you miss talking to me?" I ask.

"No," he says. "I talked to you for two months. I missed you talking to me."

I close my eyes.

"Honey, are you tired? Let's stop."

I look at him, torn between mental and emotional exhaustion and the desire to hear more, please more. "Read one more," I mouth and hold up one finger. He has developed a mantra while I "slept" with which I fully agree: Never leave anything unsaid.

I close my eyes and wish he would read forever.

11

TIM SAT ON THE END OF MY BED on another "telling me my story" day and I asked what should have been the first question I posed the moment I realized, remembered, I'd had a baby.

"Who took care of Caroline?" I asked, bewildered and slightly horrified at the oddity of days having gone by since I'd awakened, how many I didn't know, and it only now occurred to me to ask.

"For the first three weeks Kathy, Brenda, and Susan. Then Claire and Jacquelyn," Tim said. Everyone but me, I thought. "Kathy and some of our other friends asked me to consider hiring a nanny, but there's something you need to know about Jacquelyn." He told me, then later she told me from her perspective.

Jacquelyn had gone back to college that first week after Labor Day and went to as many classes as possible, then she'd lug her books to the hospital and sometimes hold sleeping Caroline on her chest while balancing her Anatomy and Physiology text on her knees.

In the time-warp of fluorescent-lit days where morning and afternoon and evening came and went as unnoticed as daylight in a casino, one thought looped through her mind.

Who is going to take care of this baby?

She knew about Kathy's generous offer made to Tim. "Tim," Kathy had said. "Let me take care of Caroline during the week. I'll bring her home on the weekends, whatever you need."

Jacquelyn knew Kathy was like my sister making her as close as you can get to family, but she thought Aunt Kathy was not, in fact, family. Jacquelyn walked around the waiting room, went into my room, took the elevator down to the cafeteria for a cup of coffee.

I do not want someone outside of this family taking care of this baby, she thought. She's our flesh and blood, not somebody else's. It's not the same to have Caroline cared for and nurtured by someone outside the family. As much as everyone has offered help and given of their time and talent, it's not the same.

Pace and think. Sit and think. Hold the baby. Get another coffee, open her Anatomy and Physiology book and think about Caroline living with someone else. That baby belongs in her own nursery that was prepared for her before she was born. The new white crib with a bead board back and a mobile stuffed lions and bears suspended from their tails was readied, perfect, against the yellow walls next to the small Windsor rocker. A toddler-sized Winnie the Pooh and Tigger waited in the corner.

That baby belongs in the home that she shares with her family, she thought, then she'd try to refocus on the A & P text in front of her, then shut it. And so it went for three days, four, and the ante upped when she overheard someone's phone conversation in the waiting room. Someone thought she already should have dropped out of school. Great, she thought. People are already making decisions for me. She knew others might be thinking the opposite, that she should get back to classes as soon as possible. What would Mom want?

She bought a cup of coffee, dumped in a Sweet'N Low and popped on the lid, and went back to the center of her pendulum swing. As loving and nurturing as Kathy's home would be, that baby doesn't belong in somebody else's home, shuttled across the state of Colorado like a sack of potatoes. She walked back to the waiting room.

Besides, she thought. A baby should not have a commute!

She sat down, sipped her coffee, and mulled over the idea that had been brewing: she could take a semester or so off of college. She tried to process the daunting idea that she could un-enroll after only a few weeks of being a college freshman. In the waiting room she walked over to Susan and Denise Chang, another friend of mine who was especially close to Jacquelyn, for their counsel. By the time the conversation was over Jacquelyn realized that dropping out of school was possible and a fairly easy thing to do, and Denise said she'd contact the administration of the school and get all the paperwork for her. As soon as it hit her that this was really an option, boom, she knew. She was going to mother Caroline for now.

Now she brought the idea to Tim. He'd been just as resolute that normalcy for her meant staying in school, but when she told him what she wanted to do he said, "Yeah, honey. That's probably a good idea."

Jacquelyn was convinced that between herself, her dad, and some help from Claire, they could do this. She knew she was young and completely inexperienced as a mom, but she thought, I'm eighteen, and . . . I'll learn this. The O'Connor baby belonged in the O'Connor home.

For Tim, concern about Jacquelyn's ability never entered his mind for two reasons—first, he'd observed her around the baby, and second, he knew that Jacquelyn had observed her three siblings being cared for as infants. Inexperienced? Yes, but he knew Jacquelyn had had a window on how it was done.

Tim and Jacquelyn finished discussing the plan, now set. "Honey," Tim said to her. "Look, you've never done this before, this'll be a big job. Raise your hand if it becomes overwhelming and we'll get a break or figure out a solution."

"I will, Dad," she said, both of them believing in, supporting, the other.

Within days Jacquelyn moved back home. Every night she'd

reach from her bed by the windows into the white bassinet for the night feeding, no question about who held night duty—of course she was going to be up with the baby, she was caring for the baby. She'd burp Caroline and put her back to sleep with a dry diaper, keep her warm, and remove extra blankets and stuffed animals when she slept. She'd asked Kathy who was constantly around, "Do babies sleep on their backs or sides or tummies?" She couldn't remember but knew it was important. "Backs," she'd said. She handled the baby without a trace of jitters, a fact that did not go unnoticed by some of my experienced friends who could not be sure if this was a young woman's overconfidence or the result of prayer, or perhaps both. Tim watched our eldest with his youngest and marveled at what she'd picked up from her view at the window.

Early in November, after Calendar Day, my friend Coletta came to visit. I have no idea at this point that she has been one of those who was constantly at the hospital or that she and her husband Craig, my older girls' youth pastor at the time, had helped prepare my kids for my expected death. They had many long talks with my kids about death and God, and getting through the first firmly attached to the second. She slept on the floor in the waiting room with others more than once, despite being eight months pregnant, spent most of September surrounding my family and me, then in October delivered her baby, Lanae, in a birthing room two floors above my ICU room. She had had a front-row seat to the drama, the "showstopper for God" as she would later tell me. But I don't know any of this yet. All I know this November day is that she's come to visit, and although she's seen me constantly since August 30th, it's the first day I have seen her since before the event.

I think she asked me questions, gently probing to see what I knew of my story, but mostly I remember the excitement and joy spilling out of her eyes and countenance.

"Oh, you are such a miracle!"

Still on a ventilator, I don't recall what I mouthed to her, but I remember doing an internal double-take. This is the first time I've heard this.

"Oh," she laughed. "You have no idea!"

No. I don't, I thought. I guess I'll have to take your word for it. I considered my fifth or sixth chest tube (with more to come) invading my chest, the tracheostomy, the feeding tube, the IVs, PICC line, and catheter, the fact that I couldn't walk or talk, and the fact that the central focus of my days was the distress of breathing. I remember looking around the room to locate the pink vomit bowl. And I recall feeling mystified at the contrast of this and her words and joy and gratitude.

Then I felt the first inkling of something I would struggle with for years: guilt that I could not muster up a reciprocal happiness.

From my vantage point, when they got their happy ending my nightmare had begun.

12

ONE DAY SOON AFTER the Sunday afternoon where Tim had begun telling me my story in earnest, he walked in for our daily visit and handed me a yellow packet, One Hour Photo Center printed on the back.

"You brought them!" I mouthed. He pulls the pictures out of the package, sits down on the bed next to me, and begins to flip through each one, narrating. The first is a shot of Jacquelyn's dorm room at the University of Colorado at Colorado Springs mid-move-in, taken a couple weeks before Caroline was born, then Tim helping assemble her dorm bunk bed. Next, me in the waiting room near the check-in for Labor and Delivery, smiling between contractions in the predawn of August 30th. Then shots of the baby, me holding the baby, my children holding the baby, one of me smiling through an oxygen mask.

"Susan, she's here!" I'd said when I called her to tell her I'd had the baby.

"Woohoo!" We'd exchanged a couple of basic details about the delivery, then Susan got right to it. "So'd you get it? Please tell me you got Tim to take a picture of you before she was born. I so wanted to see your skinny self pregnant."

"We got it," I said. "Tim took it this morning in between checking me in and waiting to be taken up to a birthing room."

"You took it in labor?"
"Yeah, see what I'll do for you?"

He shows me lots of other pictures of the baby with my children and friends.

He reaches inside the envelope to pull out the rest of the pictures and sets those pictures on the nightstand and I notice something pink next to them.

"What are those?" I ask. Tim picked them up and hands me two tiny pink felt bears. They were three inches tall with a white muzzle and a blue bear nose stamped onto their heads, eyes sewn into the felt with knots of baby blue thread, a miniature pink satin ribbon stitched around their necks and tied into a bow, and they each bore a tiny white heart glued on their chests. One had been placed in Caroline's bassinet, the other identical bear had been safety-pinned to me, and every so often the staff would switch the bears. The mother-scented bear was placed next to Caroline and the baby-scented bear was placed near me, in the hopes that, deprived of each other, that scent would bind us.

My baby could not have my voice, the sound most easily recognized and preferred by babies both before and after birth, but she had my touch, my heartbeat, and my scent. Scent connects mothers and babies before birth, as the baby's urine and pheromones mix with the mother's, changing the native scent of her body chemistry to something new and distinct. If, as it's reported, a mother can distinguish her own infant by scent alone hours after giving birth, and the mother's scent filters through the amniotic fluid, then the single sense of smell can bond; even when mother and child are separated in infancy, they may be drawn to, or even recognize, each other if brought together later in life. These pink bears were that hope.

He hands me another picture. "Here's one of when we'd take Caroline up to see you."

I look at an image of myself, comatose. I'm swollen, and the endotracheal tube comes out of my mouth and is secured in place with tape stretching around my entire face and runs along a boom over my head to the ventilator; IV lines across the left and right side of my chest are pushed apart. In the middle is my newborn, sleeping on my chest while my hand rests on her back.

I inhale suddenly and lie openmouthed. I move the picture to my chest and look away, then at Tim, and I begin to cry.

"We did this as often as we could. The ICU staff thought it was a good idea," he says. "The minute I'd put her on your chest she'd fall asleep. This day she just slept on your chest for, hmm, maybe an hour. It was a little bit of normalcy even though you were completely out. Just to have the baby with you was a little bit soothing to her. Well . . . to all of us."

I look back at the picture. The baby's cheek is on my chest, her arms prone with her forearms up, elbows at a ninety-degree angle, both of us sleeping, one on top of the other.

For a minute I can say nothing, aching for my loss of her, but mostly for her loss. Days-old babies are supposed to lie on their mother's chests, cheeks to skin, at home with their mothers who are falling in love with their babies.

With all of my babies I'd had a small ritual. After I was moved from the birthing room to the hospital room and Tim and I were alone with our baby for the first time, we would unwrap the blanket and take in the whole beautiful, tiny body fresh from mine, touch a shoulder, trace down their arm to the smallest of fingers, feet wrapped in my hand. In the birthing room I'd held Caroline close to my chest, head to head, arms around her in the cradle hold, like I'd held all of my babies. The unwrapping always came later. There would be time.

Except this time it didn't, and it never would, months later the unwrapping having already been done, irretrievable moments of fresh baby. I want to go back in time before the vent and the IV lines and the drug-induced nightmare, and hold her until she wakes like I had before, like I had when I was a real mother.

"This is the day we took her home from the hospital," Tim says. In the picture the baby is in her car seat. She's centered in the shot, he's holding the carrier, slightly to the right of the frame wearing a white shirt and a thin smile, and he's standing in front of a white wall, stark, empty, that fills the left side of the picture, like I have been erased from the shot. I see my husband in the "taking baby home from the hospital" shot, alone. Fingering the edge of the photo I see joy's absence, I see courage clutching the handle of a baby carrier.

"Tell me what that day was like," I say.

He takes the photo from me and sits down on my bed. "Well, it was midday and Jacquelyn and I began the process of discharging Caroline from the hospital. We went to the labor and delivery floor and filled out the paperwork and the staff debriefed Jacquelyn on how to take care of a baby, then she and a nurse settled Caroline in her car seat. But first I took her into your room. I wanted her to have a goodbye with you whether either one of you were aware of it, to touch you before she left."

He looks at me and tells me the rest, and Jacquelyn filled in the rest of the story later. Tim had turned to her and said, "Honey, why don't you take her home. I'm going to go back up and be with your mother."

"Sure, Dad."

They got to the front doors and Tim said, "OK, I'll see you later."

"Dad, we need to have . . . this is an important moment. We need to have a picture of this, we need to record this." Tim gave her a skeptical look. "This is a moment of Caroline's life that . . . Dad, everybody has a 'going home from the hospital' photograph. Caroline needs one. She deserves to have one too." She pulled out a camera from her purse.

"OK." He stopped at the corner of the front automatic glass doors and the white wall, held up the car seat near his chest, and just stood there.

"Dad, you've got to smile. Force a little bit of emotion. For posterity."

He smiled with his lips and she took the shot, then they hugged.

"OK, I'll talk to you later," he said and handed her the baby.

Jacquelyn walked out the doors, to the family's white GMC Jimmy, carrying the baby in her car seat across the parking lot, sad for Caroline and us that we weren't the ones getting to take her home.

At least Caroline would not be missing this picture in her baby book. Jacquelyn kept thinking about the photograph she had in her own baby book of Tim and me, young, in our early twenties, taken on the day we took her home from the hospital. I wore a white Mexican dress with red stitching and sat in a wheelchair, helped by a pointy-nosed nurse in starched white, while Tim secured her car seat into our brown Saab. I had told Jacquelyn when I'd first shown her the picture how we'd put the car seat in backward, just like The Book instructed, but when we pulled up the safety straps the baby kept disappearing. Down went the straps, down went the baby, squished under the baby neck pillow like a tiny old man bent in half, creased at the waist. We did not know what we were doing and the nurse looked disapproving and impatient and the baby kept disappearing, which got me tickled, then Tim started laughing and we laughed so hard we could hardly finish the job. There it all was, on film, us forever captured on what was clearly one of the happiest days of our lives. Jacquelyn had always cherished that photograph. And now, Caroline . . . would not have a blank spot in her baby book on the "going home from the hospital page." She had made sure.

Tim pulled out a white envelope from his backpack.

"I have some more pictures," he'd said, opening the envelope and taking them out. "These are worse. These are the bad ones." Bad enough that he'd kept them separated from the other pictures, shrouded in their own package. He held the stack and showed me the first picture. I looked, then instantly turned my head and shut my eyes, stomach tightening, exhale suspended. I shook my head no, eyes still shut. How could that be me?

"OK, it's OK. I'm putting them away," he'd said.

I'd opened my eyes and looked at him as he slid the white envelope in the inside pocket of his jacket.

"I'm sorry," I'd mouthed. "Too hard."

It had been hard to look at the other pictures of myself looking so distorted, but these pictures, "the bad ones" as we came to call them, were not images I was strong enough to look at with a breathing tube still lodged in my neck, a chest tube protruding from my left side, another one coming out of my upper right breast, a catheter between my thighs, and a G-tube coming out of my abdomen. I was encircled top to bottom, side to side, with an unspoken awareness that the woods and I were still entwined.

I wanted to look at every picture he wanted me to, to take it all in, see what he saw, understand what he felt, suffer with him just a little for what he had to go through with me while without me. I wanted to comfort him with my understanding. He didn't just want me to know what he'd been through. He needed me to know. Intently. I wanted the delayed vicarious experience of the retelling of his pain to sweep into me and remove some of the pain embedded in him, as if a tragedy only has a quantifiable amount of suffering and if I could pick up some of it he would have to carry less, feel less, remember less.

But my body reacted involuntarily to seeing my near dead self, I could feel my heart beating faster, breaths doing less work.

"I'm sorry," I'd said again. "I just can't yet."

I understood he needed to share the protracted nightmare he'd been through with the one person who knew him like no other, and he understood that looking at that nightmare—when you are the nightmare—would wait.

13

THE SUN AND I have had a long love affair. I love the beauty of morning sun streaming in a kitchen window, the feel of summer sunlight on my face or winter sun through a window, varying degrees of warmth, something akin to hope.

So, a respite from the soul-withering existence of life under fluorescent lights was the morning, where, thank God, my room had an east-facing window and early sunlight would stream in across my bed. I wanted the blinds open so the sun on my face, my bed, my room, was the first thing I saw and felt every morning, nurturing me as it always had, reminding me of the hope of another day, because I have awoken, again, each day a little miracle.

I think this little morning ritual enjoying creation as much as one possibly could, well, as much as one could sick, in a hospital bed, versus say, lounging on the white sands of St. Croix, saved me. A part of me. These first days of going to sleep at night and waking again each morning were a sheer mystery.

But those mornings also crushed me. I'd lay there for a minute or so, happy to be alive, and then a heaviness would fill me. I would remember. Morning meant I had another whole day in front of me. Another day of struggling to breathe, trying to eat, learning more about what I'd been through, trying, trying to remember, and the huge, huge amount of recovery work that lay before me that day.

Every morning in my few moments of solitude before the staff came in or the visitors arrived, I'd take in the life-giving sun, then feel the dread roll over me, as helpless to stop it as I was to pull back the covers and spring out of bed. But how could I dread another day of life that I came so close to not having? How dare I? Won't God strike me right then and there as an ungrateful slug? How could I dread the gift of a day when there was so much joy, thankfulness, praise around me and admit that I was any less thankful and joyful than everyone who came to visit? How could I dread minute followed by minute, no matter how hard, after all the torment everyone I loved had just suffered through? So I told no one.

One of my favorite things about my own bedroom is that strangers never just pop in. I can get in my bed and know that no one will be walking in unannounced except for my kids and then I can lock it when I don't want that to happen. The UPS man will not appear at my bedside with a package, my friends won't appear, my doctor sure never makes house calls, and the Ghost of Christmas Past doesn't even visit me in my bed chamber (for which I'm particularly grateful), but in a hospital it's a veritable parade and you never know who is next in line, they just show up. Boom. There they are in your room. Your life unfolds at the whim of everyone else. Well, I realize whim isn't exactly the right word to describe the schedule and medical plan that a plethora of specialists and rotating shifts of nurses carry out in order to help heal you, but the view from the bed is that life happens to you.

One extraordinarily difficult aspect of illness, especially long-term illness, is the loss of control in and over your own life, which is somewhat of an illusion in real life, nonhospitalized life too, philosophically and spiritually speaking; nonetheless, having no say or usually any warning of who is going to walk in your door or when or for what is disconcerting. In the real world you can say I'm going to go get a double shot mocha latte and you have decided that you will walk in the doors of Starbucks when you decide to, you'll see the baristas in their green aprons, they don't just waltz into your bedroom with a coffee. Choice, which is different from control, having a say in who we choose to populate our day or whether we choose to take a different route or eat Chili's takeout or skip a meal or see a matinee or go to Target or work until midnight, is a beautiful aspect of life. Hospital life is a mash-up of endless tedium and the Unexpected Parade of the Unknowns. Today's parade brought another nurse through the door.

"Hi, I'm here to get you ready to go down for a chest X-ray," she says.

"Now?" I ask.

"Yes, now. Transportation will be here in a few minutes," and she begins the process of moving tubing, readying me to be moved into a wheelchair and rolled down the corridor, down the elevator, into the basement radiology rooms.

"I'm going to unplug you from the wall oxygen to this tank," she said as she worked.

"My daughter's coming. Can we wait please?" Claire was on her way to come visit.

"No, they're expecting you downstairs." Yeah, but I wasn't expecting them, I wanted to say, but didn't because your expectations and desires for any notification or warning, any say, are irrelevant in this rabbit hole. You fall in and new rules are at play. Or so it seems to the patient.

"Well when she gets here could you tell her where I am and help her find me? I'd really appreciate that." I didn't know how long she could stay and did not want to miss her visit. This was not a world in which she was comfortable.

"Oh sure."

I think I remember double-checking that she would make sure that Claire found me when she arrived.

Tubing snakes into a coil in my lap, blanket over my knees,

oxygen hitched to the wheelchair, we make our way downstairs and into the small, dark room for the test. They lay me down, bring the large machine over my chest, and do their work. I lie still. Breathe in. Breathe out. I shiver. The machine is very close to my chest, all I remember is being sandwiched between cold metal, a cold room, dwarfed.

Breathe. Breathe. The pressure in my chest builds.

A female tech came in telling me something about not being done or someone needing to look at it or they'd have to do it over, it doesn't matter what, all that matters was what happened next.

She pulled the door slightly closed, leaving it open a crack so I could see the hallway light and I strained to listen to the footsteps that passed in the hall, listening for Claire.

Breathe. Oh why is it so hard to breathe? I took deeper breaths, longer breaths, trying to force more air into my lungs to satisfy the need for more air. Still I waited, captive, cold.

Where is everyone? Footsteps in the hall, but none for me.

What if they've forgotten me! Panic began to rise in my throat and fought with the escalating need for air, more air.

"Hello? . . ." A person can only whisper so loud.

"Hello? Anybody there? Is anybody there?" The raspy whisper floated through the crack in the door and fell on no one's ears.

I was alone.

I hungered for more air, hurt for more air. Calm gave way to tears, then I tried to control the tears to better focus on breathing.

"Help, someone help me please." I listened to see if I heard anyone in the hall who'd heard me. "Help," I'd whisper again. Breathe, breathe, whisper for help, repeat. Breathe, breathe, whisper for help. Repeat. I wondered how long I'd be able to do this before I wasn't able to do this anymore. Then I'd cry.

It takes very little time, seconds really, to move from comfortably taking in oxygen to needing more than you've got.

Footsteps in the hall again.

"Help me, please."

Footsteps stopped, did an about-face, and the door cracked open more.

"Mom?"

"Claire. Claire."

She was at my side.

"Go get someone," I whispered. She bent down next to me. "Go get help," I said. "I can't breathe." Shock passed over her face, then she was out the door like a flash, bringing with her a nurse or a tech squeaking her soft-soled shoes on the linoleum as she whirled into the room and over to me.

"I can't breathe."

The woman looked at the dial on my oxygen tank.

"Oh my God."

She unhooked my plastic tubing from the tank and quickly tapped into the oxygen spigot on the wall. Life-giving, panic-easing oxygen began to flow again through the plastic and into my lungs.

Disconnected from the endless supply of oxygen at the wall in my room for this little field trip, dependent upon a portable and temporary source from a canister, I'd been left alone with an oxygen tank that had completely run out.

Amazingly, that happened a second time, although with less dramatic circumstances. After that, until the day I left the hospital, I refused to be unconnected from the wall source and connected to portable oxygen without seeing for myself that I had, like a car, a full tank or a spare.

14

"WE'RE GOING TO BEGIN weaning you off the ventilator tomorrow." A nurse turns to Tim. "Can you be here?"

"Absolutely."

"We've found that it's helpful, especially in the beginning, if a family member is here."

This should have been a tip-off.

The next day the respiratory therapist arrived and explained the mechanics, that we'd start with a short amount of time of reducing the ventilator, short trials of switching from air being pushed into my lungs with a heartbeat-type regular rhythm, to me breathing naturally, if you call breathing with an oxygen cannula in your nose natural. My lungs would be doing the work instead of the machine. If all went well, they would gradually increase the amount of time during each daily weaning session that I'd spend off the vent. When that session was over they'd reconnect the vent until the next day, and eventually the vent is nothing but a bad memory and you are breathing what's known in hospital settings as "room air."

That they use the term "weaning" is rich with meaning. When my older children were infants I nursed them until the time I decided that they were ready or I was ready for them to stop nursing, which was a different amount of time for each child depending on the child. An extra bottle or sippy cup here, a jar of pureed plums there, more and more mashed potatoes off my plate, and gradually as that all increased, the less time we spent in the rocking chair nursing, until one day, and I never knew when that time would come, one nursing session would be the last. Increase one form of sustenance, decrease another, add time, and eventually the baby, or the patient, is weaned. Milk, air, same principle. Except this one involves a teensy bit of terror.

The next day, with Tim at hand-holding distance, they unceremoniously unhooked the ventilator tube from the trach tube in my neck. The sound of the vent stopped. It was my lungs and all that room air, the anticipation and hope was palpable that the two would find each other and mingle.

If there's one thing, and there's more than one thing, that I'd like the medical profession that works with ARDS patients or anyone on a ventilator and the patient's family members to know, it's this: try to understand, find out from those who've been there, what weaning from a vent can be like for the patient.

I instantly panicked and wanted the vent turned back on. I flashed back to a scene in the James Cameron film *The Abyss* where a white rat was submerged in a tank to breathe fluid instead of air and thrashed around during the transition from one way of breathing to another. That's how weaning felt, like liquid breathing. The respiratory therapist and Tim would coach me through the sessions, like labor, and afterward I'd cry and my hands would shake. I went through days of weaning sessions before I was told that my psychological reaction (fear and tears) was not uncommon. Eventually, the distress faded and room air was all I needed.

Day after day now, Tim would walk into my room and share another tidbit of my story. "You metabolized the drugs so fast the nurses couldn't believe it," Tim said. "Several of them kept saying they'd never seen anyone metabolize medication so quickly."

"How could they tell?" I asked.

"Well, for one thing, your pain level."

I let this sink in for a moment. I demonstrated pain in the coma? I wasn't just a sleeping body in a bed?

"What would I do?"

"Move your arms and legs, grimace. And you'd try to reach for your breathing tube. One of the nurses called you Amazon Woman," he said.

"Amazon Woman? Why?"

"Because they were surprised that someone so small could be so strong. You'd pull against the restraints."

"What do you mean restraints?" I asked.

"At one point they put your arms in restraints. To keep you from pulling out your ventilator tube. And they'd have to increase your sedation. The restraints weren't constant, just this one period of time."

My body tensed at the thought of imagining my wrists secured against the metal bed railing.

"Another nurse called you Pocahontas, with your long dark hair across the white pillow."

I imagined what she saw and had the strange sensation of seeing myself asleep, as if I were floating over my own comatose body, as my mind worked to see, to experience, to make sense of the story they were telling me of myself.

Kathy came to see me almost daily too and fed me story morsels, one of which has changed my perspective on one of my fears I've always had for my children.

Near my daughter Allison's birthday, my friend Becky had emailed Kathy asking for our home address so she could mail a birthday present she'd bought for Allison. Becky and I had started our friendship as writing and speaking colleagues and had grown into sister-friends, who knew and loved each other's children, and she had wanted to get something special for Alli's tenth birthday. She stopped in at The Mineola Mercantile, an East Texas boutique not far from where she lived, and told the owner what had happened to me and that I was lying in a coma missing my little girl's birthday.

The woman told Becky she thought she knew "what God wanted this little girl to have."

She pulled out a silver charm bracelet and three silver charms—one said "Big Sis," another of a heart with "mother and daughter" written across the front of it, and finally a letter "A" with a guardian angel peeking through the "window" of the letter.

The store owner said, "Now tell little Alli that charm represents her guardian angel that is always watching over her all of the time." Becky went home, wrapped the present, wrote Kathy for the address, and only when Kathy replied did Becky discover a fact she had not known when she'd bought the gift.

It had been my tradition on each of my daughter's tenth birthdays, their double-digit day, to give them a silver charm bracelet.

I'd given Jacquelyn one, Claire one, and was looking forward to giving Alli hers.

Such a thing. Comatose for months; tradition intact. Unthinkable. I'd been learning since my awakening, and would continue to learn, how well my children had been cared for by Tim, one another, and family and friends, but at that moment, all I could think about, what I've never forgotten since, was that despite my unspoken prior fear of what might happen to my children if I was ever taken from them, my child was loved with a love more powerful than mother love. Coincidence? Perhaps. But I don't think so. Loved by her God? I believe so. His eye was on my sparrow. And I've not been the same since.

On a mid to late November day, Jacquelyn walked in for a late afternoon visit. Her long dark hair hung nearly to her waist, her figure slim, casual, clad in jeans and flats, she was the picture of a beautiful, vibrant eighteen-year-old, save this. As she entered room 401 she toted a diaper bag on one arm and the plastic infant carrier seat, full of two-and-a-half-month-old baby on the other, creating a contrast of youth and too-early responsibility that filled me with conflicting emotions of gratefulness and sadness, joy and guilt.

"Hey, it's Mama," she said as she walked in. "Look who I brought," she said to me, smiling, setting the infant seat on the end of the bed. I pressed the up button raising the back of the bed higher to see the baby.

Now that I was awake Jacquelyn brought the baby much more often and for different reasons. Before I was awake she'd come for herself and for Caroline's sake, so the baby could be in the presence of her mother. Jacquelyn had wanted to someday be able to say to Caroline if I'd died, "I took you to see your mama while you still could. You don't remember it, but you did spend time with her." Now she brought her to help my recovery and to help me bond to my baby.

"It's nice to meet you," I kept wanting to say every time the baby and I were together. We'd look at each other with a mutual "you look like an OK person" matter-of-factness and, well, hang out.

Until a whimper or squirm or scowl indicated a need and I'd look to Jacquelyn for interpretation. "She's probably ready for a diaper change," Jacquelyn would say to me, or to her, "Oh, Caroliney" (they were now on a nickname basis), "it's naptime, isn't it?"

When a look of consternation crossed Caroline's face, it hit me—I had no clue what mollified her. Jacquelyn, with wisdom beyond her years, did not swoop in to take the baby from me and give her what she knew she needed. Did this baby tolerate a horizontal arm holding or did she need to be held upright? Did this cry mean "my tummy hurts" or "feed me" or "burp me" or "bounce me please"? Was it a sway or a face-out position that calmed her cry? A finger stroke on the curve of her temple?

"What does she like?" I'd asked my eldest daughter about my youngest, realizing I did not speak this infant's infant-maternal language, but she did. She picked her up instantly and swayed in a way that soothed this baby, our baby.

This November afternoon Jacquelyn had her dressed in clean, matching clothes, tiny baby socks, a baby outfit wholly un-familiar to me. I didn't know if it had a spit-up stain on the right front requiring extra Spray'n Wash or had come from Target or in a gift bag, didn't know if it was the only outfit in blue or the tenth. She was a pleasant baby, lying there in a strange outfit, a stranger to me despite our family and friends' efforts for it to be otherwise.

My mother-impersonating daughter unstrapped her, lifted her out of the seat, held her up for me to get a good look.

"There's Mama," she crooned, holding Caroline to face me. "Say 'Hi Mama. I'm such a good girl. I don't cry or fuss.'" I raise my eyebrows at Jacquelyn. "She doesn't, Mom, she still doesn't. She only fusses if she's hungry or wet, Mom, she never cries."

I smile. She never cries. What a gift. I look at my daughter taking to mothering like she was born to the task. To hear Jacquelyn talk and to look at this tiny package of a human as pleasant as the first sunny spring day, she seemed bestowed with a quiet, a peace, a countenance that not only tolerated changing environments, and multiple caregivers, days on end of trips to the hospital instead of trips to the park, but also a countenance that eked joy out of weary, dry, hospital-saturated souls.

Jacquelyn stood near me, holding my baby, and told me about her and Caroline's day so far. Caroline squirmed, chirped baby sounds, looked around bright eyed, then screwed her face into a tiny protest of hunger. Jacquelyn looked tired. She sat down in the chair at the end of my bed facing me, cradled the baby, tucked the blanket around her, and fetched a bottle out of the diaper bag, feeding her and talking to me. We had a good visit and settled into that easy quiet where you're just glad to be with one another and a lull in the conversation is as easy as sliding into a perfectly broken-in shoe. Jacquelyn held the baby, burped, patted, jostled her until Caroline's limbs went limp in sweet sleep, then this sister-mother leaned her head back against the wall, closed her eyes.

I watched the two of them, amazed at their individual beauty and the enmeshed beauty of these two daughters, flesh of my flesh, now life-giving to me, and each other. How could she do this? How could I not? I watched them for long minutes, looked at that sleeping baby, that beautiful, round-faced, dark-headed stranger of a baby in my daughter's arms.

"Jacquelyn."

She opened her eyes, blinked.

"I want to hold her. Would you help me hold her?" I had to hold her. Never mind that she'd fallen asleep. I ached to hold her. An ache that was new and raw and good. A longing, deep and fierce, to mother this baby I could not mother.

"Sure, Mom." She stood, walked over to me with baby in one arm, and reached for extra pillows with the other, which she wedged under my elbow against the bed rail. I was able to move my arms around the baby, stroke her face, put a bottle in her mouth, but hold her in my arms, just my arms? No. Completely deconditioned means completely lacking strength, muscle tone, ability to hold one's baby unaided. With the pillow supporting Caroline's weight and chest tubes and stomach tube tucked aside, we nestled her as close into the crook of my arm as possible, scooched her close, her chest and tummy and cheek against me, against my empty breast.

Awake now, she squirmed and started to whimper. Jacquelyn patted, cooed, tried to settle this baby into peace in my facsimile of an embrace. We propped up the bottle and Jacquelyn stood next to us, watchful that I was supported enough not to drop the baby and the baby was content enough not to rattle the mother. When she was still and sleeping, Jacquelyn sat down in the reclining chair and in minutes was asleep. New mothers always need more sleep.

I looked at this baby, held this baby, felt an emerging warmth flow over me like heated syrup drenching pancakes. No one came into the room. An unusual quiet prevailed. Minutes turned into half an hour and the baby slept, a half hour turned into an hour and I watched her still, felt her breathe against me. I didn't want to move for fear of breaking the spell of this moment, the amazement and realization that I was capable of feeling something for her, anything.

Pain escalated. I know it's easier to manage pain by staying on top of it than it is to let it go and then regain control. Like a gas stove flame rising from simmer to low to medium, from warm, to warmer, to bubbling, you catch it, yank down the flame before you get to burning and out of control.

My pain heats up, simmer moving to low, creeping to medium, and I ignore it, focusing on this baby next to me. The longer I can ignore the pain, the longer this suspension of time with this child will last. It is not that I am captivated by mother love, by falling in love with my baby, it is not just that I'm afraid once I crack the seal allowing others into this moment, even others who will bring me pain relief, that the spell will be ruined, this special, private connection will be over. It is all that, and this. A dread and unspoken fear.

I drink in the pleasure of this sweet hour and a half where the hospital room hardware has faded away until there is just this baby on a pillow, touching me, and that is all there is in the world, as if we were rocking in a down-cushioned rocker at home, in a pink nursery with *Brahms for Baby* playing softly, a vanilla candle burning, framed pictures of family scattered about the room.

I stay here as long as I can, then the pain pushes me out of this place and I wake up Jacquelyn to help summon a nurse. Soon there is flicking of the syringe, liquid gold, flowing into my IV, and near instant relief ratchets down the flame. I hold her until I can't hold her another second, look at Jacquelyn, nod, acknowledging it's time to give the baby back to her sister-mother. She takes her from me, lowers my bed, and I close my eyes, the spell broken, and let the drug have its way with me. As sleep came, a hazy fear settled on me like a falling fog, a fear that the baby ache that had washed over me, the longing I'd felt, as sharp and visceral as any longing I've ever had in my life, might not return. The fog thickened, as fogs will do, but it did not drench, could not drown out, the contentment I'd known for those sweet ninety minutes.

15

FOR A LOVER OF BOOKS, long stretches of time with nothing to do but read are anticipated, savored, then remembered; we plan for them when we can, enjoy the pleasure of the feel and smell of a book, get lost in the story, then enjoy the sustained pleasure that comes afterward, thinking about the world we've just been to or the people we've just hung out with on the page, in the way a good book lingers like the aftertaste of a fine wine. One would think lying in bed, with nothing to do, nowhere to go, hours and hours and days and weeks stretched out as blank as canvas would be the ticket to hours and days and weeks of reading bliss, the upside of a hospital address. Unfortunately one of the side effects of a coma, not to mention oxygen deprivation, is a hit to your vision and concentration and mental processing.

For the longest time I was so sick I didn't have the strength or inclination to read, but looking at my books stacked up on the bedside table was comforting, like having old friends sitting in the room with me, friends who didn't require anything of me, friends who brought me great pleasure just with their presence, waiting until I could engage with them again. They were a minuscule reflection of the soul-sustaining acts my family and friends gave me, but bibliophiles know the inanimate pleasure of the friendship of books.

In the early days of regained consciousness and the adjustment of deconditioning I'd reached for my Bible. It might as well have weighed a hundred pounds. I cannot lift my Bible, I thought, shocked, nor could I read it. The words and lines blurred, came into focus, then ran together like ink in the rain. I closed it.

The hospital chaplain came around fairly often to visit me, a retired gentleman with a charming nature who shared my love of books, and one day he walked in carrying a brown bag from The Tattered Cover, Denver's famous independent bookstore, from which he pulled out a copy of *Cold Sassy Tree* by Olive Ann Burns and Henri Nouwen's *Life of the Beloved* and *The Way of the Heart*. I marveled that he'd gone shopping for me and I tried repeatedly to read them, but the lines would not quit dancing, except by effort I could not sustain, and the words, once read, were like vapor in my mind. I used to be a writer, I thought. Now I cannot even read. Those days are over, I thought, and lay thinking of who I'd been, wondering who I was now.

One afternoon Tim told me what had happened in my in-between, five days after my one-day awakening and move to the new hospital on October 15, and before Calendar Day. "You nearly died again. Kidney failure," he'd said, and this made fear sidle up and try to take up residence in my bed. Yes, I'd been through so much, yes I was alive (which is really a miracle any day for all of us), but I was still on life support. I'd had a medically induced coma, but I still had ARDS, lungs that could not adequately oxygenate my body. I realized and felt how ill I still was, and thought, I could still die. A chill of mortality made me feel fragile, like a bone china cup at a demolition.

Why was I afraid? Because I wasn't faithful enough? Brave enough? Maybe. Or maybe just because I'm human. Years later when I learned that death from ARDS after awakening from the medically induced coma is not uncommon, I remembered this eerie afternoon.

Most days, however, were even stranger than that afternoon of fear. Most days my constant companion was a staggering degree of peace. The kind you read about. The "passes all understanding" kind. And this still amazes me as much as it had that first meta-cognitive moment in November when I'd realized I wasn't asking "Why, God?" It's an astonishing phenomenon to have one's life smashed upside down, families and mothers and newborns separated, suffering high and answers low, a demeanor that appears to some as depression but which is in reality severe illness . . . and yet, still lie in a hospital bed and marinate in peace.

Someone knocks on the door.

"Hey." Brent peeks his head in the door. "You feel like a visit?" he asks, stepping into the room.

"I do." I turn my wheelchair around and he pulls up a chair next to me to sit at eye level, which, after holding court from my bed, looking up at people most of the time, was almost disorienting talking with someone eye to eye.

"So how ya doing today?"

"Better. I can talk."

He smiles.

I'd received a Passy-Muir valve, a device that allowed me to speak while still receiving mechanical ventilation. Normal breathing through the nose and mouth allows air to travel through the upper airway, facilitating taste and smell and—as it passes through the vocal folds, speech. A tracheostomy tube is inserted in the neck below this and air bypasses the upper airway, thus preventing speech. (Other complications while keeping a person ventilated can occur too, including secretion problems requiring suctioning, and with loss of taste and smell, appetite can diminish and compromise a patient nutritionally, as it did me.) When I received this valve—which closed at the end of inhalation and before exhalation, allowing air to pass through the upper airway again, and . . . ta-da, to pass through the vocal chords (glory!)—I could speak again.

The woman who inserted it had finished and said, "Try it out. Say something."

What do you say when you haven't spoken in months?

"Hi . . ." I thought for a second. "Thank you."

Then I called Tim at work, but since he was away from his desk, I had to leave a voice mail. He saved it for years.

The sound of my voice almost startled me. It was different, scratchy, weak, but gloriously audible. It seemed only fitting, since I'd woken to a different body than the one I went to sleep with, that when my voice came back it would belong to the new, weak, suddenly old body. They matched. But I didn't care. The changed sound was odd to my ears and I couldn't talk for long without getting tired, but I was deliriously back in the business of communication, and sitting now with a friend and conversing, voice to voice, is a very beautiful thing.

Brent and I talk about his vantage point of when the sleeping and waking began and a frightening night in mid-September. Just before my pain stops us, he looks at me and says, "Did Tim tell you what he did that night?"

"What do you mean?" I ask.

He pauses. "I better let him tell you about that."

16

BREATHE IN. BREATHE OUT. Concentrate. Ignore the pain and do it again. My chest aches, the compression ratchets up as I watch the minutes click off on the wall clock across the room, feel my chest tighten, then begin to feel and hear each breath. Like a scuba diver. I lay still, listening to and working for each breath.

I want to call Tim, but he is back at work now that I was out of the woods. He understood like no one else the hellish ride my body had gone through. He knew every twist of that roller coaster, the horrifying plunge to the bottom to just miss death, dips that leave you breathless, blind turns that rattle the soul, free-falling into critical illness, and now the slow trek up. I just want to tell him that today isn't a good day.

We're not supposed to think about breathing. One of the amazing feats of the human body is the ability for the lungs to expand with oxygen-rich room air, send the oxygen to our alveoli, where it works its magic and sails along into our bloodstream oxygenating organs, systems, energy, our life. Meanwhile we exhale the toxic carbon dioxide cast-off, and do it all over again, some 18,000 times a day, every day of our lives. And we don't even think about it. Cheers to our medulla, our brain stem pilot light. It's kind enough to bypass conscious thoughts of breathing, leaving us free to consider what we want for dinner, when we should pick up the dry cleaning, and where we should go on our vacation, to dream of possibilities and reflect on how soft and scraggly and warm our husband's face was this morning under our fingers. Unconscious breath is one of those rare gifts that's best enjoyed when we're unaware of it. All's not well when breathing shifts from its involuntary, incognito nature to compete for mind space with more pleasant thoughts of grilled salmon and Pinot Noir, Cancun, tomorrow's potential, this morning's sensory goodbye.

I'm not alarmed about the pain. This is yet another day where I hear the portable X-ray machine seconds before they turn into my room, then sit me up and place that cold metal plate behind my back.

"Breathe. Deep breath in. Hold it."

Ka-chin.

"Thank you."

Sit me up. Take the plate. Wheel out the lumbering piece of metal that opens a window into my chest for a map of today's fluid path and the size of today's pneumothorax—those holes in lung tissue that transmute breathing from oblivious gift to conscious burden. That displaces thoughts of how good it will be to see my children this afternoon and that tiny leap in my heart I get when I hear two, three steps in the hallway of boots scraping polished linoleum, knowing who they belong to before the man they hold appears. When those boots pivot into my room, my day is changed.

No. Those thoughts yield to musings of how odd it is that I have tubing extending from my chest and elsewhere and how hard it is to try to make myself stop thinking about how much it hurts, the tube, the breathing, the whole sorry mess. A quiet little civil war right in my head. Boots scraping . . . tube pushing . . . the wine with dinner I'll have when I get out of this place . . . take a deeper breath even though it hurts . . . my baby's soft skin, the sight of my kids' faces . . . breathe, breathe, breathe.

I tell the nurse my chest hurts.

"I'll see if it's time for more Dilaudid," she says.

Before she returns, another nurse walks into my room with results from the X-ray. Highly unusual. They tell me my lung has collapsed. Again. I need another chest tube and a trip downstairs. Now.

I call Tim's cell phone but it just rings. Insistent on being informed, he'd cautioned me to tell him before any procedures. I tell the nurse I'll wait until I can reach him.

Instead I find myself being wheeled downstairs for an emergency CT scan for a pin-point placement of the chest tube. Seems my left lung is 95 percent collapsed on my heart. I'm in danger of a heart attack. One minute I'm in my room counting ceiling tiles and breathing, breathing. The next minute I've activated a small swarming army. I ask them to keep trying to reach my husband before they proceed.

They scan my chest. "Did you reach Tim yet?" I ask.

Not yet.

They check the image. They have to reach him before they make another hole in my body. "Don't let them do any tests until you call me," he'd said.

The radiologist leaves the anteroom, comes over to my body half sticking out of the cylinder, and gets close to my face, whether to comfort or convince me of the gravity of organs collapsing over other organs, I'm not sure.

"Lindsey, I'm Dr. R."

I like him. His voice has an unusual mix of control and warmth.

"We've got to get your lung inflated quickly," he says.

Lying flat exacerbates what feels like a pile-on of sumo wrestlers but without the sweat. Oxygen flows through my cannula faster than it did in my room. Breathe. Breathe. But there is no breath deep enough to satisfy or lift the sumos. Hunger for oxygen and my husband fill me.

X marks the spot is drawn in purple on my skin. Still no Tim.

Someone says, "We're still trying to reach your husband." They double-check where they'll place the tube through my chest wall so near my heart. It's all done in that quick, efficient, exigent way I'd come to know. With a long hospitalization or a medical battle waged seemingly without end, one begins to become cavalier about yet more tests. But there are far too many people involved now to feel calm, their controlled soft voices incongruent with their pace. My pulse quickens. I suddenly realize that this is beyond my new normal of breathing irregularities and repeat chest cavity invasions. My lung is almost totally deflated. My heart could seize at any moment. I begin to shake. Lying on cold metal, surrounded by the expert flurry, I feel utterly alone, in that chilled place of distress when only the one we love the most can comfort our soul.

A nurse sticks her head out of the room behind me.

"We got him!" she says. "Your husband's on his way."

I close my eyes and feel the urge to sob. The cavalry is en route.

Dr. R. gets close again. He tells me he's got to begin. He cannot wait for Tim to arrive. He talks to me in a way meant to assure me of his skill, which it does, and he pats my left arm.

"Do you understand?" he asks. I nod.

A nurse gives me another dose of Dilaudid and Valium. One for the pain. One for the fear. I feel the momentary liquid warmth as the drugs begin their magic.

"Is he here yet?" I ask. I picture him driving so fast his taillights leave red contrails like night photography of old Chevys dragging Main. No. Still not here. I wonder if a person can will themselves not to die, if you can will your heart to keep beating, until your loved one arrives. I've since come to believe that sometimes this is possible. A grandmother staves off death for weeks, the extended family is sent for, then gathers, and hours after they arrive, she's gone.

A nurse, one who's been touching, patting me in reassurance these last minutes whenever she walks by, bends down and whispers near my ear.

"Those meds should be starting to help," she says. "Your husband's almost here."

The room feels icy and I shiver from its cold and from teetering at the edge, again.

They're about to start, the staff has all moved behind the protective glass and I'm alone now. I hope I'll hear some voice over that loudspeaker telling me that Tim's arrived. All I hear instead is the soft whir of the CT machine, noises of invasive procedure prep, dimming voices. Then a heavy ca-lick, ca-lick, ca-lick. I hear familiar boots scraping polished linoleum and then the cavalry is there, bending into my ear, grabbing my hand.

"Hurry," I hear someone tell him. "They're starting."

He kisses my temple and is escorted out as fast as he raced in.

Who knew that in the middle of an emergency in a radiology lab of a top trauma hospital that a team of scientists and highly trained technicians had a heart for a love story?

Looking back I wonder at the tremendous tension of those moments and I'm not sure why I was so frantic for him. Was I just trying to be the good wife? He'd said don't let them do another procedure to me unless he knew and he was there. His sense of knowledge, and at times control even, amazed me, he'd earned every ounce of my trust. Somewhere beyond reason I may have thought if he was there he could control it, control the outcome. His commanding presence would size up the situation and preside. That heart that beat for him wouldn't dare stop.

Then again, if they invaded me without his knowledge and it went south, the whole mess would, of course, be my fault. So delusional are we in love and crisis. Maybe the sense of desperation was the fear that after surviving so much for so long, our quota of approved prayers had run out and how could we expect to come through yet one more critical care crisis? If this was going to be the day when *breathe, breathe, beat, beat* replaced thoughts of my baby's breath and that faint look of hope and apprehension on my kids' faces when they'd walk into my room, thoughts of warm sand and salsa music and salty margaritas with the husband of my youth . . . if this was going to be the day when *breathe, breathe, beat, beat* drowned out all of that, and God's answer to today's prayer wasn't a rescue boat but a bridge to the other side, well, I just wanted to hear that boot-scraping gait that changed my day one more time.

We all want to connect. With that person who's got our ticket. Who knows who we are in our hidden places. Maybe this connecting in ordinary days that wake to coffee and conclude with a kiss and amazing days that sear our memory, connecting in days of bliss or fear or worship or fights or making love, maybe this connection is one of the most perfect gifts we have in a flawed world, a prelude of a mystery to come that we cannot imagine. Maybe this connection, during distress, this comfort, is as vital as the air we breathe.

Emergency abated, I wake up as they wheel me into my room, wince in pain when they lift me from gurney to bed. The air in this room is different than in the one downstairs. It's easier to breathe because all the tension has drained out. I look over at the figure stretched out in the chair. The cavalry has his boots up. I close my eyes and sleep.

17

PERSONAL SUFFERING (is there any other kind?) is a great leveler of mankind, and in our best moments we endure suffering with nobility, grace, transcendence, and let character shaping do its work. In our worst moments we wallow in self-pity even while we loathe the said self-pity mid-wallow. In the meantime between the two, we can cry and grit our teeth and smile and pray, pray, pray we will survive it and pray, pray we will be of use to someone through this and after this and wait for the IV magic juice and grab our loved one's hand. Did I mention praying? Oh, and besides doing all that and thinking about what it feels like to be a feverish five-year-old whose mother eases our misery with the touch of her cool hand to our hot cheek and a gingerly, expert placement of the wet washcloth on our forehead, we can also squish up our suffering in a metaphorical wad and say, "Here, God. Use it."

Memoirist Patricia Hampl writes in *The Florist's Daughter*:

Even pain—physical, mental, you name it, all forms of anguish, misery, any plight or pity, all injustices, losses and humiliations, all the meanness you're likely to encounter in this life (because don't think life will be *easy*, girls and boys)—all of it has a purpose. *Just offer it up*, Mother would say, echoing the nuns. *Offer it up.*[1]

She describes observing childrearing on display by some mothers in restaurants, demonstrated by "fashionable, preternaturally patient mothers leaning down to their imperious three-year-olds. *Do you want the California roll? Would you like the calamari? Sweetie, what would you like?* Give the kid the mac and cheese and tell him to offer it up."[2]

And that's what it boiled down to. In and around my prayers and tears and hand-holding and magic juice I found my greatest comfort when I managed to offer it up.

Like my mother would have done, like any good mother, my friend Brenda broke down the daunting, the impossible, into minute increments although I didn't see it that way then. But I did notice that she bridled the tiny tasks with motive, the impetus for me to face another day's mountain.

"Here. I brought you a smoothie," she said. She'd come a second time from Houston to visit me. Once for my family while I was unconscious and now for me.

"Thank you." My stomach tightened and rolled. "I really don't want it."

"I know." She dipped the spoon into the frozen cream and held it to my lips. "One bite," she said. I complied.

She picked up the book she was reading to me, read for a couple of pages, then grabbed the smoothie again.

Eat because the nutritionist says you must. Eat because Dr. B. said, "Right now malnutrition is your biggest problem." When he said that, I'd fingered the right chest tube, the left chest tube, and felt the ventilator's constant swoosh of air down my throat and wisps of cold air that swirled around the collar encircling my neck. Constantly. How could malnutrition be my biggest problem?

"Alright, Dr. B., I'll try," I'd said. And I really did. But how could I know, how could anyone know who hasn't experienced it, how difficult it is to make yourself eat when eating is work? When it's the biggest challenge of your day? When the very thought of food triggers an uncontrollable gag reflex or vomiting.

"Have another bite," Brenda said. She brought the spoon to me and I shook my head no.

"For Caroline. Do it for Caroline."

I teared up and she waited. She'd found the one place where my defenses and will, my self-preservation and excuses, fell away, useless to me now, in the light of the power she'd tapped. She'd tapped into that force that I could not deny of a baby needing a mother and realizing that unfortunately this baby's mother was me.

I opened my mouth, accepted her bite like a baby bird, and another one, and another one, no matter that my stomach rolled. "Do it for Caroline," she said and those words, that idea, lodged deep inside me looping in my mind, as they would for years to come, the fuel behind so many things I could make myself do no other way.

There was no nonstop ticket from the MTU floor to the train home. The desired departure to my longed-for destination required a mandatory layover on the rehab floor, nontransferable, nonchangeable. Fourth floor to sixth floor, constant care to the rehab, physical therapy, prove-you-can-function, work-your-butt-off floor. The day I moved was like graduation. It took a couple carts and trips for Tim to haul my accumulated possessions to my new digs and before leaving there were goodbyes and thank-yous to the staff I'd come to know. I was moving up, literally and figuratively, well enough to get the heck out of Multi-Trauma Unit, for a trial run before being sprung. I never understood why women could have babies and be sent home almost immediately regardless of the fact that they had preschoolers at home and could really have used an old-fashioned long hospital stay, and cardiac patients could have open-heart bypasses and be sent home within the week, but I was in Leavenworth. The move upstairs was my last stop before freedom and I was thrilled.

Until I got there. The new room was depressing. It faced the heliport pad and every time the life-flight helicopter took off or landed I wondered if the patient was going to make it or not. The staff was new, no one knew me, nor did they seem to want to, I felt. The transition from being known to unknown is jarring, whatever the circumstances. And one of the most trivial aspects of my move, but deeply affecting, hit me full force on waking up the first morning. My previous view of a courtyard lawn banked with white-trimmed red brick walls that had allowed me to daydream it was an English manor where I was an invited guest or some other nonsense, and the healing, morning sun that had fallen on my bed, was now replaced by gray rooftop and no direct sun at all. Just me and fluorescent light. This made me a little cranky.

They explained that every day I was expected to get dressed. No lounging around in sexy open-backed hospital gowns for me. Get up, get your clothes on, eat that dadgum breakfast, and wait for physical therapy, then your trip down to the gym where I was introduced to a five-step flight of stairs to nowhere that might as well have been Everest. This was boot camp, baby. Do the work or, bam, back downstairs you go, passport denied.

On this floor it was me and the geriatrics. Buddies. We'd shuffle down the hallway pushing our walkers on our way to group exercise class or the gym, nodding to each other as we passed, with our oxygen in our noses and our pulse oximeters on our fingers. I could only imagine that a healthier version of us would have us shuffling down a Florida boardwalk on the way from bingo to our 4:40 dinner, the women with blue hair, the men in black knee socks, white shoes, and Bermuda shorts, and me. I'd gone to sleep a forty-one-year-old, woken up old, and here I was on the geriatric floor to prove it.

The first day in my rehab room, though, I'd found a piece of white paper on my food table, mistakenly left, intended for staff, listing all the patients on the floor, their names and room numbers, their doctors, I think, and what I vividly recall—their diagnoses. I scanned it and saw my name. In the diagnosis box I saw "Anoxia." I read it again.

When Tim arrived I asked, "What's anoxia again?"

"It's a lack of oxygen in the blood cells or tissues that can cause brain damage."

"Why'd they write that instead of ARDS as my diagnosis?"

"I don't know. Mistake? . . . Well, that is what they thought you had."

I sat on the edge of the bed, dressed and waiting to go down to the gym for stair climbing and ball balancing, waiting for the physical therapist, and instead Tim's face brightened my door. His smile peeked over the top of a glass vase spilling with tangerine roses.

"Hi!" I said, grinning.

"Hey you." He walked in, set the flowers on the bedside table, and leaned over and kissed me.

"You brought me flowers!" He grinned, looked at me a few seconds, one hand hiding behind his back.

"Do you remember what today is?" he said.

"What's the date?"

"November 28."

I rolled the date around in my mind, coming up blank. I looked at him, squinted my eyes trying to think.

"And this, for you," he said pulling his hand in front of him to show me a bottle of Martinelli's sparkling cider and a pink envelope.

"What's this?"

"You don't remember?" His eyes shined a little, watching me in this role reversal. I don't think there'd ever been a day in our marriage when he remembered an event that I'd forgotten. November. No birthdays. Our anniversary was April.

"Flowers, a card, and champagne?"

117

"Well, it's that fake sparkling stuff. I'd hate to get you this far, then kill you with alcohol contraband."

"Too bad. I wouldn't have told."

"Told that I'd brought you contraband or told that I'd killed you?"

"Neither one. Our secret." We laughed.

"Where do you keep the good glasses around here?"

"In the bathroom."

He disappeared into the bathroom and emerged with two plastic cups, set them down, and opened the bottle. "You give up?"

"Yeah, I give."

"Today," he said, enjoying the moment, looking me in the eyes, "is the twentieth anniversary of the day I asked you to be my wife."

I just looked at this man for a few seconds, pushing down the lump in my throat, trying to figure out who he was and what he'd done with my husband. We'd gotten engaged the night before Thanksgiving. He'd done the whole ask-my-father's-hand-in-marriage thing without my knowing it, and had taken me to The Glass Menagerie restaurant, with live piano music, champagne, Caesar salad prepared at the white linen–covered table, his knee hitting the floor when he pulled the black velvet box from his jacket. It wasn't an anniversary remembered by date, and we weren't ones to mark non-anniversaries as anniversaries, but it was one we remembered every Thanksgiving eve, whatever date it fell on each year. Even so he'd never given me flowers on Thanksgiving eve. Or cards. Or champagne.

He poured the sparkling cider into the cups while I opened the card, then he handed me my cup and raised his.

"To twenty years. And to the next twenty."

We clinked plastic, smiled at each other, and took sips.

After he'd left I stared at the flowers and the card I'd propped up on the side table. The card kept falling so I put it in the drawer. That afternoon I opened the drawer, pulled the card out, and reread it. Put it back in the drawer. Then I opened the drawer again, read the card again, tucked it away, until a few hours later, when I opened the drawer again.

Home for Thanksgiving, home for Thanksgiving, home for Thanksgiving. It had been my goal since Calendar Day.

"Can I go home, Dr. Fenton?" I'd ask my pulmonologist.

"We'll see," he'd say, like a father patiently answering a child without promising anything. We'll see, we'll see, we'll see and suddenly Thanksgiving was a week away, then three days away, then tomorrow. And I got . . .

A pass.

A twelve-hour layover stamp on my passport, no overnight stops allowed.

Tim arrived that morning, smiling at getting to spring me, however briefly. I'd been so excited I hardly slept the night before. Had wheelchair, will travel. Check portable oxygen. Double-check portable oxygen. And we were off.

The ride home was the first time I'd been in a car in almost three months. The transition from months of immobility and solid walls to now hurling down I-25 at seventy miles an hour was terrifying. And thrilling. But mostly terrifying. My stomach in a knot, I fought the urge to keep my eyes shut all the way home. And then I was. All the way home.

We drove down our gravel S-shaped driveway and pulled up to the house, the sand-colored porch, rustic white posts, red front door, welcoming me, embracing me in the way that a home that you love does when you've been gone and then you return.

My children stood on the porch, waving with big grins, and greeted me like I was the Queen of Sheba or Helen of Troy returning from vanquishing the land at long last. Alli jumped up and down when we pulled up. Tim maneuvered me in my wheelchair and the oxygen tank up the stairs, and I absorbed my children around me on my front porch, near speechless with joy. In the kitchen I looked at them gathered around the island as if I'd just left them there a few days ago, looking comfortable and in place, looked at Tim and took in the sense of all of us, together, in the kitchen, as it should be, as it used to be. For a moment I forgot all about the wheelchair and the oxygen. I was home.

The house was immaculate and readied for the holiday, our family's favorite. An extra table had been set up in the kitchen with an olive tray and cheeses, a turkey roasting in the oven, the table set, all like a magazine photo shoot. I ate two olives and a bite of cheese and the memory of tasting that briny tang and creamy cheese still makes my mouth water. I was sick later by the time the family gathered for the feast and I couldn't eat, but no one has ever enjoyed an hors d'oeuvre more than I did then.

Home about an hour, I moved from the wheelchair to the sofa when Jacquelyn walked into the room and set something down on the floor next to me. I looked over the arm of the couch and there sat an infant seat, holding my infant.

"Look who's up," Jacquelyn said.

"Oh." I looked down at this beautiful child who looked around the room as if she knew the place, belonged.

"Mommy's home, Caroline. Look. Mommy's home," she said in a genuine, connected, non-saccharine, mommy-crooning voice.

"Oh," I said again. I smiled. "Hi there." I'd been home an hour, had eaten, talked, reacquainted myself with the comfort of my leather sofa and wide plank wood floors, the view down the valley out the den windows, the sound and space and feel of being in my own home again, being with my family. I looked down at her, this first moment of laying eyes on my three-month-old baby at home in my house, and tried to look casual, calm, but wondered if anyone could tell that for the hour I'd been home, I'd forgotten I had a baby. It felt a little like walking into a room after you've gotten a new armchair that you've wanted for a long time and at great expense, but accustomed to the room before you got the chair, you're a little surprised to see it the first time you walk into the room with the new addition in place. I reached down to touch her, amazed at the odd sensation of pleasure at seeing her and shock at the realization of forgetting her.

Thanksgiving night my day-pass was over and I had to return to the hospital. My father and stepmom were still in town and the whole family had visited me several times over the holiday weekend, but one day Dad came to hang out with me, just the two of us.

"Daddy, I'm so glad you're here," I'd said.

"I'm glad to be here. Just to be with you." He sat in the green vinyl chair, his leg crossed over his knee.

"Daddy, I'm so sleepy." It was only noon. "I don't think I can stay awake."

"Well, you just sleep. Get yourself a little nap. I'll just go down and get a cup of coffee."

"Daddy, I'm sorry."

"Don't be sorry. I need a cup of coffee. Would you just go to sleep so I can go get me a cup of coffee?" He smiled and leaned over and kissed me on the forehead. "I'll be back." He waved, walked out, and when I next opened my eyes there he sat, expecting nothing from me but breathing. That afternoon he took me for a "walk."

"What do we have to do to get out of here?" he asked.

"Well, we have to unhook from wall oxygen to the portable thing, and just tell them where we're going to be."

"You feel like going for a walk?"

"Oh yeah." We got some help, signed out, and blew that popsicle stand.

He rolled my wheelchair down the hall, down the elevator, onto the first floor, and he walked the halls with me, up and down.

"How you doin' today?" he'd say, nodding, smiling, as we passed patients and visitors and doctors. There are no strangers in my dad's world. He rolled me outside, around the triangle of sidewalk by a towering Colorado blue spruce tree where patients often went to get outside, the lucky ones anyway, and we walked until we were too cold in the late November air to stay out any longer. We passed a patient standing outside smoking. "I just don't get that. Hooked up to oxygen, smoking," he said, shaking his head. He wheeled me back into the building.

"Where's this hall go to?" he asked.

"I don't know."

"Let's go find out." He walked faster, then a little faster.

"Hold on, here we go," then he broke into a little jog, and there I was, flying down the hallway, surprised, laughing, "running" with my father, like the old days when he'd take my hand and run with me across the sand into the Galveston gulf and lift me over the waves, again and again, laughing.

"You all right?"

"Yeah!" The air moved across my face and arms, through my hair, feeling wonderful, alive.

"How ya doin'?" he said to a few people we sailed past in the hall, some who looked astonished at seeing a grown man running with an invalid grown daughter in a wheelchair, but some smiled at us. One thing my father has always taught me, without once ever putting it into words: You don't wait for happiness to come to you, you take it in every snatch you can.

18

"DR. FENTON, can I go home yet?"

"Not yet. You still have fluid in your lungs. Let's see how they look in a few days."

"Dr. Fenton, can I go home yet?"

"I'm seeing some improvement in your X-rays, but not enough to be comfortable sending you home yet."

"Dr. Fenton, can I please go home?" I must have asked every day. Thoughts of home became constant. I wanted to climb into a bed without a motorized back and rails, into clean 500-count sheets across from the stone fireplace in my bedroom, the one that I shared with my husband. Used to anyway. I wanted to walk from room to room in my house, just because I could, because I belonged there. I wanted to walk to the fridge, open the door and stare into it, enjoying the fact that it was there, before 7:30 a.m., 12:00 noon, and 4:45 in the evening. I wanted to sit on my porch and walk into my study, lie on my sofa, feel hardwood floors and soft carpeting under my feet, smell the smells of my family, my home. I wanted to walk into the nursery and look at my baby asleep in her crib, a sight I hadn't seen yet with this child. I wanted to see my children comfortable, happy in their own four walls. I wanted to climb in bed again and lie next to the man I loved. I wanted to watch Tim standing at his bathroom

sink lathering Barbasol over his stubble, catching the faint whiff
of Soothing Aloe, watch him pull the razor down his cheeks and
up under his chin. I wanted to wipe the little smidge of shaving
cream from the base of his ear that he always misses, like I've
done a million times. The night following the night I'd dreamed
and sensed evil, I'd been so shaken I'd had him spend the night
with me, sleeping on that insufferable hospital fold-down chair,
my sentry, my knight, and the next morning I'd watched him
stand at the hospital sink and lather Barbasol. Did I call him to
my bedside, ask him to lean down so I could wipe the dab he
missed? Surely I did. What I remember was the longing to live
with him again that watching him shave evoked. It's funny how
life's unremarkable moments can be the artifacts that tether us
to the essence of a person.

"Dr. Fenton, I really want to go home."

"We'll see. Let's get some more X-rays."

So we got some more X-rays, until I practically glowed. Every
day my pulmonologist, who I'd developed a tiny crush on in the
hero-ish way that really sick people come to view their favorite
doctors, would walk in my door, discuss the state of my lungs,
why I was still nauseous and had been every day since I'd woken
up. We talked about "sats" and hemoglobin and hematocrit
levels and pneumothoraces daily, the way liberated people talk
about dark roast coffee with cream and mocha cappuccinos as
normal morning conversation, throwing around words casually.
I so wanted to talk about cappuccinos.

Another day. "Dr. Fenton, can I go home yet?"

"By Christmas. Why don't you plan on being home by Christmas."

He left and a black cloud that had been gathering steam rolled
over me and unleashed, capturing me in its torrent. Christmas.
It was early December. He left the room, I lay back down in my
bed, dressed for the day in stretchy knits that were not a part
of my old wardrobe, pulled the covers up to my chin, then over
my head, for hours. Because hours was one thing I had more
than enough of. Which if I were grateful, and appreciative, and

spiritual enough, I'd have joined everyone else in praising God for these hours, because the alternative is that your current hour is your last, there are no guarantees on your next hour, ever, as long as we all shall live, and I knew that. And I was grateful. And I did praise God. As much as I was capable of for someone who'd missed the drama, had slept right through the nightmare that those around me had to live through, slog through, suffer through day after horrible day, and I'd not only missed the drama they witnessed and were characters in, I'd missed the climax of the whole tragedy. I'd woken up, albeit a couple of times, finally stayed awake, and had not just survived the seemingly endless sleep that is life in a coma, had beaten death, but had been given a miracle of life when life in the face of medical probability is utterly below betting odds—impossible. A miracle at the hand of God. A miracle that could not be explained any other way. A miracle because people had prayed, and God had said yes. A miracle that I'd missed.

I was as grateful as a person could be who is told an amazing story about someone else. You're glad for them, really glad for them, and at times your heart gets full with the amazement of the intersection of a human life and God and the mysteriousness of him showing up and doing stuff that we glimpse or grasp or feel. But we feel most deeply the things that involve us directly. This was their miracle. They'd seen it. They'd prayed for it. They'd sweated and suffered and endured and prayed and sweated and suffered and endured some more and then witnessed what some of them had called a "showstopping act of God." I'd woken up and been told about it, in a dribbling of information because I could not handle very much at one time, had tried to catch up on the story and grasp it, then retain the events, the timeline, the players, the emotions, the details, and the overwhelming drama of it all.

So, yes, I was grateful, as amazed by God as we can be when we hear about his affairs in the lives of others, trying, trying, to be as grateful and amazed and full of praise as they all were. But this day, the wait-until-Christmas-to-go-home day, gratefulness and amazement and praise curled up in the bed beside me, climbed under the covers with me, and lay quietly next to my chest tube leaking with fluid, keeping me company while I cried and contemplated the heaviness of the suffocating cloud and the length of an hour.

———

"Dr. Fenton, can I go home yet?" Maybe I could wear him down out of sheer frustration at being asked the same question every single day, like he was keeping me there because he had nothing better to do.

"I'm just really not comfortable with that yet. Let's see how your X-rays—"

"Look tomorrow," I finished.

"Dr. Fenton," I said the next day, "you have got to let me go home. I can't take it anymore." He looked at me, like he really heard me this time, was weighing what I said against his medical opinion that I wasn't ready to leave. I still had a chest tube protruding from my lungs. Reluctantly he agreed to give me a trial run and write an order for the tube to be removed. If my sats dropped we'd have to reinsert it (which would have been an eighth time), and did I understand this? Yes. I did. Anything to get the chest tube out. I'd have to stay for twenty-four hours after they took out the tube and if I passed, then I got the coveted stamp in my passport, "discharged." But not without dire warnings of all that could go wrong, a lecture of the warning signs of danger and instructions for what to do if I felt chest pain when I got home. (Answer: do not pass go, do not hesitate, call 911.) I nodded, agreeing to everything, to anything to go home, completely unaware that ARDS survivors sometimes reach this state of healing then succumb to fluid in their lungs from which the worn-out alveoli cannot recover and after surviving near death multiple times, rousing from their drug-induced comas, getting off a ventilator, talking with their families again, getting better, they then get worse and still, well, die. I heard his warnings, but I did not know this shocking ARDS fact yet.

126

Even if I had, I still would have been greeting Dr. Fenton with my tiresome refrain, holding my passport out, begging for the stamp that would send me packing from a world I hated to the one I knew. Home. My old life.

The next morning they took the last chest tube out, my sats held for twenty-four hours, and there I sat on the edge of my bed, waiting for Tim, dressed for travel, passport in hand. He carted my stuff to the car and came back for me where I sat ready in my wheelchair, and we unceremoniously, unhesitatingly left. We drove out the circle drive in front of Swedish Hospital, pulled out onto Hampden Avenue, and I looked up as we crossed under the sky bridge at the people walking across and noticed a patient in his wheelchair looking out the sky bridge windows onto the street filled with traffic. I felt both torn with sadness at that person looking down and thrilled to be one of the blessed ones in the cars below.

The highway speed gave me vertigo and I felt like we were flying, tearing down the road going a thousand miles an hour, risking death every second, so unaccustomed was I to motion.

"Have you heard this song yet?" He turned up the radio and Sheryl Crow sang "Soak Up the Sun." "It's new, got real popular while you were asleep."

"See that?" He pointed to a building nearing the end of construction. "That's new. I've watched them build it while I've been coming to see you." It was almost a whole new building existing now on my way home from the hospital that didn't exist when I'd made the trip to the hospital. Surreal.

We pulled into my gravel drive and stopped in front of our long porch. It struck me that I needn't watch the clock to return to the hospital. Tim helped me out of the car and I stood for a moment and took it all in as the kids ran out to greet me with posters they'd made inked with colorful markers that said "Welcome Home Mom!" and signed by many of our friends.

"You're home!" they said. "You're home!"

We sat at our round wooden kitchen table, Sonic number

twos and fries and cherry limeades and Dr Peppers in front of us like a feast.

I'm home, I thought. I'm home; Dorothy, done with Oz.

The first few days were tenuous. A home health nurse came daily to dress the last chest tube wound and assess my lung function and oxygen saturation and repeat instructions of exactly when to call 911. The comfort and familiarity of home covered me, vaguely disguising the thin layer of serious doubt about my ability to stay there, forty-five minutes from the safety of hospital staff instead of four seconds. Tim and I were sobered, knowing I was precariously close to not being quite well enough to have left the hospital, but we weren't fearful, in the way we might have been if we'd understood just how many ARDS survivors are so not out of the woods at this point.

Everything was the same and everything was different. My fridge held food anytime I wanted it, which was still almost never, but that didn't matter. I lay on my sofa, looked at the mountains from my den, stared and stared at my children, felt soft carpet under my toes, and best of all, climbed into my own bed, touched the coolness of my own sheets in a bed without a rail and with a husband. But all of the familiar was new.

I had left this house young, walking under my own power, strong. I had been plucked out and returned, like a time warp, speeded up thirty-five, forty-five years, now rising from the sofa and moving across the den floor by scooting with a walker. The juxtaposition of the old me in my home and these first days of this new me in my home disoriented me, as if the hospital had been a transitory existence. A large box-shaped condenser, the size of a good-size suitcase, hummed day and night with the oxygen I needed constantly. A fifty-foot line of tubing gave me mobility to go from room to room downstairs and when I needed to nap, which was often at first, or go to bed at night, which was early for a long, long time. Tim would help me upstairs, then move the condenser. The constant hum of the machine, the clear tubing winding around my house, trailing me, the walker, the riser and rails installed in the bathrooms, were so very out of place connected to me, in my home, these tools of an old person, the person I'd become.

One evening Tim and I are in our room.

"Honey, are you ready to look at the rest of those pictures yet?"

I look at him.

"The bad ones," he says.

"Nope," I answer.

Tim gave Jacquelyn and Claire money to go buy Christmas presents, which they did, then they tried to involve me in the modified festivities in the sweet way one might try to engage your visiting elderly grandmother who arrives for a holiday.

"Mom, you want to help me wrap presents?" Jacquelyn asked.

"Yeah, that's a great idea." We sat at the dining table, the one where I'd wrapped piles of presents when she was five. She wrapped a present, I cut my sheet of paper. She wrapped another present. I pulled off tape and stuck it on the end of the box. She wrapped another present and I finished my first. Then I was spent.

"For this next exercise I want you to grab onto the table." A new physical therapist came to my home three days a week. "Hold on, steady yourself, and I want you to raise up on your toes, as far as you can." She demonstrated steadying herself with one hand on the dining table while smoothly rising to the balls of her feet, heels high in the air, balancing tiptoed, then smoothly lowering herself to a flatfooted stance. I grabbed the edge of the table, raised up on my tiptoes, or tried rather. In my mind I rose up on my tiptoes because how hard is that? Except I didn't. My heels lifted less than an inch. I tried again. Lift. Rise up. Tiptoe.

"Why can't I do that?" I asked, slightly shocked, which by now I certainly shouldn't be, but then, this was the first new-old body instance in which I'd been asked to tiptoe, thought of trying to tiptoe, and that's just something that your brain assumes you can do, what with being able to do it since you've been seven months old.

"Because that's what happens when you've been completely deconditioned."

There was that word again. And not just deconditioned, but completely deconditioned. "You have to rebuild muscle, a little at a time. It'll come," she said. "You've got to give it time." Before the coma, never enough time. Since the coma, nothing but.

My favorite thing about mornings now was waking in my own bed, looking out the northwest windows at the distant view of the sun on Mount Evans, knowing that if I'd had a bad night I could take a nap, guilt-free, and that no one would be coming that day to draw my blood or take me for an X-ray. It's the small things in life one savors, like not being stuck with needles and shot full of radiation.

Mid-mornings meant my exercises, and the business of eating, which was still a great effort, filled a chunk of minutes, but those early days involved a lot of sitting. Sitting on the edge of the bed, sitting at the table, sitting on the sofa, until it was time to go back and sit at the table. I'm a terrible TV watcher. I shake my foot and get bored quickly and, with some exceptions, usually think of the book I could be reading or project I could be doing, which was a little problematic because all that sitting wasn't filled with lounging in front of the TV nor could I concentrate on my book or do a project. In fact, it was the doing that was the problem. Life at home, like the hospital, involved a lot more being than doing. When you strip away the ability to do work, you are left with three things—your family, yourself, and God—and I was given the amazing gift of trying to figure out how to relate again to all three.

130

Be with your family. Be by yourself when they are busy doing, doing almost all of the things for you that you used to do. Be with God. Be present. Be in the moment. Be still. Just be. Which compared to the alternative of not being, meaning being dead, is a dead-on good deal. Sometimes, when I'd watch my family laughing or my baby sleeping in her infant seat, gratefulness at this gift welled up until it washed all over me like a cresting wave in an ocean of joy. Sleeping next to the man I love, after so many months of sleeping alone, sitting at the table with my family, after so many months of a tray over a bed, nourished the fiber of my being.

Getting dressed in the morning in those early months home was a strange affair. I discovered, my first day home actually, that even a toilet riser, a plastic seat attached to a normal toilet to make it higher, and handrails around the toilets of the elderly and infirm, require a certain strength even among the feeble to be used independently. On that first day home my husband had helped me maneuver my walker into the bathroom and left, until I called him back, shocked that I was incapable of standing from even a raised toilet. The flesh on my thighs appeared to be covering useless muscular tissue, what there was left of it, like window dressing on femurs. Arm muscles were also deteriorated past the point of strategic use to assist the thighs. He returned and lifted me up. We looked at each other soberly. It was going to be a long road. "I'm sorry," I said, looking away from him. We'd always been as comfortable with one another, as intimate, as two people can be, but not being able to attend to personal needs, relying on one's still young husband to care for you in such intimate matters like you are a child crossed some barrier in my mind. I'm supposed to be his lover, I thought, not this.

The strangest part of my morning routine was facing my image in the mirror. I'd had long hair almost all my life and now I stared at a head with cropped hair, a forced cut in the hospital from months of lying on it, hair that had no luster, was beginning to fall out, so much that I began to fear washing my hair because I would pick up a fistful from the drain afterward, and it fell out eventually in clumps like a chemo patient. It would take weeks, just days I felt, before I would be bald, to learn one of my medications had a side effect of alopecia and that ARDS patients often experience great hair loss during their recovery.

The face of the image in the mirror was altered, pale from almost four months under fluorescent lights, round from the massive steroids, rendering me nothing like I remembered myself. Applying makeup gave a strange effect, like the not-quite-right look of a child with painted and mascaraed eyes or an old woman with ruby red lipstick. I'd look at the stranger I saw, walk away, and remind myself, "I'm still in here. No matter what that mirror says, I'm still in here." I'd walk away, trying to replace the image I'd just seen with the one I remembered, trying to find a way past the visual lie, past the atrophied body, past the uselessness of purpose I felt, to my core, my soul, that does not depend on appearance or use. A soul loved by God. A soul loved by Tim, by my children. A soul that because of these things, I could make peace with again someday. I kept telling myself these things believing the telling would bear fruit.

When you have been away from home for a long time and you return, things you usually never noticed before stand out and I found myself enamored with accoutrements that normally blend into the background of a busy, full, normal life. A pre-illness life. Like my stainless steel refrigerator. And my kitchen sink. You never realize how big a kitchen sink is and how nice it is to just go stand at, until you have stood before a tiny bowled hospital sink for months and brushed your teeth by spitting in a pink vomit bowl before that. Granite tiles and cherrywood cabinets and towels with bleach stains that you put there, bathrooms without emergency call strings and red panic buttons. All of it stood out in relief against the memory of an institutional life.

Since August 30th the family's meals had included takeout

food, Tim and the older girls cooking, restaurant gift cards given by people (fabulously helpful), and catch as catch can, but mostly meals arrived from church families. Neighbors and people from Tim's work had also provided food, but three or four times a week the church brought food, as they continued to do for the first two months I was home, an amazing, life-giving almost six months of care and feeding.

One of the first times we went out to eat was a Sunday after church. We walked into the Black-eyed Pea for fried chicken with mashed potatoes and gravy, fried okra, finally free to be out in public dining as a family. Along with leaving the house with oxygen, I had to take a cushion to sit on because my back end was still withered like an old man's and sitting down was basically sitting on bone. Cumbersome, but still liberating and we were growing used to our paraphernalia. What I wasn't used to, what indeed shocked my sense of self, was a stranger's comment that day.

We walked through the restaurant's crowded foyer and as we passed I heard a woman say none too discreetly to her husband, "Look, honey, she's so young to be on oxygen."

I'd been able to upgrade from a walker to a cane, and while she'd said I was young to be on oxygen, what struck me was the image of what she'd seen to say that. Silver oxygen canister, cane, cushion, old-man rear end. Earmarks of my new very-old self, walking with my young-looking husband. I was embarrassed to be so old, embarrassed for a young, handsome husband to have a suddenly elderly wife. He'd never made me feel that way, but I suddenly saw how others must see us. Old and crippled with young and able. Saddled. That's what he was, I thought, that's what that woman must have meant. He's saddled with her.

I followed my family to the table, ordered okra, and pushed back my growing burden, like the burden I was.

Living in the hospital, as people with long-term illnesses do, is rather different than the usual stay of several days or a week, takes getting used to and is undergirded with a constant desire to not be there, but by and large one does get used to it. I had learned to figure out the rhythm of the days, what to expect, the staff's job and my place. Now, having achieved my constant desire of coming home, all that changed again, which was of course an incredibly good thing, but was like starting a brand-new game with new rules just when you'd gotten the hang of the old game. The new game had to be learned by the whole family. We spent the early days after my return home figuring out the new rhythm, what to expect, whose job was what, whose place was what, all of which was outside the bounds of the typical family hierarchy.

Someone had to be home with me constantly for a long time which meant each day Tim and the older girls would discuss the family's schedule, something that for almost two decades had been my domain. I'd been sidelined from this role for almost four months now and they'd figured out how to function as a family unit in my absence, but hearing about it in the hospital was altogether different from watching them run the family in front of me. I was grateful and proud of them, in awe at times, but it was also strange. So much had changed since I'd been gone. Old roles? Poof. Was I the child needing to be babysat or the great-grandmother needing elder care? I was the un-mom mom. When Tim was home they went to him with questions. When he was gone and Jacquelyn was home, she was the alter-parent, except when she shared the duty with Claire or they tussled for bits of it.

I felt the unique combination of amazement at their adeptness, but also a sense of displacement. I felt a little like a much-anticipated visitor. The family member you love and have been waiting to see and are so glad they're there, but as a visitor, they fold into your lives. It's not their job to take out the trash or plan the meals or say "Yes you may go to your friend's house."

I felt no need to jump in with any suggestions or directions in the beginning. I watched in amazement. It was a testament to their character, their adaptability, their strength, work ethic, and love. It was also a testament to the countless people in our church and community who helped pick up the pieces of a family, patch holes and soothe souls with the hundreds of things it takes to smoosh a fractured family into a cohesive, functioning unit. And it was a pulsating testament of grace being lived out before me. God's grace visited on seven people.

I'd been spending a lot of my sofa time holding Caroline and feeding her a bottle, changing her if the diaper bag was nearby. One afternoon the younger kids were at a class, Tim was at work, and Jacquelyn and I sat upstairs in the loft just off the nursery talking while the baby slept.

"Oh, she's awake now," Jacquelyn said and jumped up to walk into her room. I watched her fly out of her chair, dart out of the loft and into the baby's room. Like I used to be able to do. Hear your baby. Respond. Zip. Zip.

I listened to Jacquelyn through the open door coo to the waking baby, "Hello, Carolina. Did you wake up? Did you have a good nap?" It's funny how instinctive the mother-to-baby-coo can be and Jacquelyn had it down at the perfect pitch. I stood up, reached for my walker, looped the oxygen tube in my hand for slack, and walked to the nursery, then stood just inside watching Jacquelyn. She'd reached into the crib and was stroking Caroline, straightening her outfit. "You're soaking. Let's change you," she said heading for the changing table. "Then we'll get something to eat. Are you hungry, Carolina?"

I watched her lift the baby, carry her toward the changing table, something I could not do. I was not strong enough to lift her yet and even if I had been, I couldn't have walked holding onto a baby and a cane. That moment, watching my daughter rise at the beckoning call of the baby, so swiftly, so reflexively, and moving to pick her up and take care of her immediate needs of a dry diaper and food, I realized that all my holding her in the world would not make up for what Jacquelyn was doing. Caregiving. More specifically, bonding through caregiving. I don't think I'd ever realized, until then, that so much affection, so much heart connect, happens when we take care of someone.

In Elizabeth Gilbert's memoir *Eat, Pray, Love*, she wrote about contemplating having a family before her first marriage ended. "But did I have a responsibility to have a family? Oh, Lord—*responsibility*. That word worked on me until I worked on it, until I looked at it carefully and broke it down into the two words that make its true definition: the *ability to respond*."[3] I'd had the family, had undertaken the responsibility, but when I read her words I thought back to this loft moment. That's what I'd been missing then. An ability to respond. To respond in full anyway, or quickly, or most important of all, to respond by myself, to something as simple as a baby's wakening noises signaling fresh needs.

Jacquelyn glanced at me near the open door, looked back to Caroline, one hand never leaving the baby, the other reaching for a diaper, like she'd done it a million times, then did a double-take and looked back at me.

"Mom," she said, her voice soft with recognition, seeing what must have been wistfulness in my eyes, loss, trying not to show through. She stopped reaching for the diaper and looked at me, with knowing and more tenderness in her eyes than I'd seen before in my eighteen-year-old. "Do you want to do this?" she said. I don't think I answered or could say anything right then, but she didn't wait for an answer. She picked up the wet baby and a stack of diapers and wipes and walked to me, past me, into the loft. I followed and sat back down in the rocking chair. She handed Caroline to me, set up a makeshift changing table next to me, went back into the nursery for a moment and returned with Desitin and Johnson's baby lotion. Then she went downstairs to the kitchen, made a bottle, and brought it to me.

I'd been brought a bottle to feed her before, had been handed a diaper and a wipe, but this moment was different. It was tinged with my surprise at recognizing that tending to the physical needs of someone was more than just loving them, doing what you need to do because they need it and it's your job to meet those needs, it was in the ordinariness and repetitive tasks of this tending that you fall in love with your baby. It was a moment of sadness that this is one of the many things that had been missing for the past four months, still was. And it was a moment when my eldest daughter recognized without words that this caregiving was as essential to me as it was to Caroline. More so at this point in time, because care was something Caroline had in spades. She'd been tended to, cared for, changed, fed, burped, talked to, loved on, carried about, and admired since she was born by a houseful and a church full and a family full of people who could scarcely bear that this newborn had been deprived of her mother. Plus, she was a particularly charming, beautiful baby, or so I've been told. So Caroline didn't need me to care for her; I, however, needed to do so.

I sat in the rocking chair, pulled off a wet Pamper, swabbed and lotioned, changed and fed and burped and rocked from my manufactured caregiving station, created just now by one daughter for another daughter. A small change, a slight transition packed with meaning. With my altered ability to respond, we'd recognized the need to alter the environment and the responder, so I'd have some ability to respond, my eldest stepping back so I could falter forward.

There was nothing I could do about all those months of my missing tending except begin where I could, how I could. There was no making up for lost time, no cramming in as much care as I could to hurry the bond, because 107 diapers could not erase 107 days of being MIA. There was just beginning here, now, at this moment and in this condition, which was a convoluted amalgamation of lament for what was gone and hope for what was yet, of sadness and faith, and letting myself miss what was lost, mourn what was lost, feel the loss without fear I'd break or she'd break or we'd all break or that God would somehow think me less because I dared to look at loss and acknowledge it for the gaping black hole that it was.

A few days later I walked into the kitchen and stood at the counter surveying my former domain. Cookbooks on the shelves, staples in the pantry, Soft Scrub and Joy under the sink, unmade meals lurking. I stood there a moment, alone, realized there was nothing for me to do in here yet, and walked back into the den. I'd had enough of the sofa—you can only sit on your own sofa as a visitor for so long—so I kept walking. I walked into the library, scanned the one wall of floor-to-ceiling shelves filled with books. Every time I picked up a book I'd read a couple of pages until I either got a headache or got sick of trying to keep the lines from blurring together. What is the deal? I wondered. I turned around and walked back into the den. The sofa won.

Later that day someone helped me upstairs and I walked into my office off our bedroom. The book I'd been writing in August lay somewhere in the piles of papers and stacks of books and embedded in my computer in a file, somewhere, all untouched since the last days of August. I walked to the desk and ran my hand over the dark red leather notebook that had been my daily companion and command central for my schedule, to-do's and projects, phone numbers, notes, and repository of creative ideas. For years I'd taken it almost everywhere I went. It was how I knew where to go every day or what I needed to do next and kept me from being later to places than I already usually was, and we were as close as twins, this leather book and I, it was my alter-brain. I flipped it open by the plastic bookmark I'd always kept at the current day's page.

August 30, 2002.

The day time had stopped for me.

I flipped it closed. Turned and walked out of the room.

What should I do?

I had no idea what room to go into next.

19

I DON'T REMEMBER the first time it happened, but I should, because this strange phenomenon happened repeatedly and for the longest time and it unnerved me at first.

Shortly after I'd gotten my magical Passy-Muir speaking valve, I called my friend Becky on her cell phone.

"Hi, Becky, it's me."

"Lindsey!" Then her voice cracked. "Hold on, I've got to pull over." She began to cry.

The first time I went to church, people came up to me, a few of them with glistening eyes. I saw another friend who was visiting from out of town. She saw me and burst into tears. "It's so amazing to see you standing here, alive." This teary-ness on sight happened with another friend, and another. I called another friend to thank him for praying for me, our first conversation since the ordeal, and he broke down. Then it got really weird. A woman I didn't know but who knew me saw me in the grocery store and she began to cry.

Wow. I'm a human onion.

It's disconcerting for your very presence to suddenly cause people to cry. I was taken completely off guard the first few times it happened and didn't know if I should hug them or stand there or tell them everything was fine or I didn't know this mattered that much to you, that I mattered, or why. Should I say it's not that big of a deal, please don't cry, or it was a huge big deal? You can't possibly know the appropriate thing to say in an odd circumstance you've never experienced before when you don't understand what's behind these reactions. The common refrain was, "You're a miracle! I'm looking at a miracle." And it felt as perplexing as if someone had looked at me and said "You're a saint" or "You're an alien" because I know neither one is true but they're standing in front of me having this genuine emotional experience that my presence triggered. Why? I kept asking myself. When people who love you see you and cry it's a good thing. The soldier comes home finally, the lost child is found, reunion destroys the tension of separation and joyful tears need no explaining. But this continued to happen with people to whom I was not particularly close, or did not even know, exacerbating the strangeness, accentuating the fact that I was the trigger, but the cause was entirely beyond me, unrelated to who I was as an individual, connected to an experience they all shared that I did not. They had been following the months-long story as it unfolded and they had prayed, asking for a life-and-death miracle, and now, standing before them was not just me, it was an in-the-flesh connection to the ethereal, spiritual, so often intangible world of prayer and their part in it. They seemed to be responding to an embodiment of an answer to their prayer.

Gradually the strangeness of the onion response stopped being so strange, people would often apologize for crying and I'd say, "It's OK, this sort of happens a lot," my attempt to offer comfort and connection, and they'd talk about what it was like to stand in front of and talk to a miracle. I responded by agreeing, because how could I not? Shifting the focus off of me and onto God and their connection to him because of the result of what they saw before them seemed infinitely more comfortable and right. Whether or not I was comfortable with people saying "You are a miracle" seemed beside the point, trivial, and anything other than complete agreement was not an option, bordering on tinkering with someone else's miracle, or blasphemy.

When we go somewhere we have never been, if we possess the least bit of curiosity, of which interesting people possess in spades, we will ask, "What was it like?" So much of life is homogenized; a Starbucks in Denver is identical to a Starbucks in New York City, here a Walmart, there a Walmart, everywhere a Walmart. So discovering someone has been someplace I have not, that's different, unusual, or new to me, is good reason to expand horizons, whether a hole-in-the-wall locale or an extraordinary experience, and so it was with me. After all, a coma is a place in the sense of a state of being, a state of consciousness where one lives for a slice of time, and it's an experience, both uncommon.

One afternoon, it might have been the first time I went shopping after I'd recovered enough to venture out, I walked into a local bookstore to buy a gift. I was casually acquainted with the shop owner. We called each other by name and discussed the book business sometimes when I shopped but that was it, we'd never talked more personally than that. I pulled my oxygen tank behind me, the green-topped silver tank on wheels, in the days before I got the type of oxygen I could strap over my shoulder, and scanned the books. The owner saw me and walked over and greeted me.

"I heard about what happened to you," he said.

"You did?"

"Yeah, we prayed for you."

"Thank you so much," I said and we chatted for a minute or so.

"Hey, do you mind if I ask you a question?" he said.

I adjusted my oxygen cannula that wrapped around my ears and into my nose, trailing in front of me into the tank like a geriatric fashion accessory, which rather made thinking about a good or bad hair day a moot point, and told him sure, ask away. We had stepped back a little out of the main aisle, cocooned a tad by the shelves of books which lent the conversation an almost conspiratorial feel.

"What was it like to be in a coma?" he asked.

I took a deep breath.

"Do you mind me asking?" he said.

I didn't. But which part to tell? The sudden descent? No, that was simply one minute you're here and the next minute you're knocked out. The long stretch of nothingness? What was it like, what was it like? I grappled with putting the experience into adequate words.

"Well, most of it was like a very deep sleep," I said. The very deepest, darkest, longest sleep, that shuts out awareness of outside time and the life you've lived and the people you've loved, and there is nothing but a complete lack of consciousness, an existence devoid of experience, thought, feeling. Nothingness. Death within life. People of faith understand and believe in the concept of life after death, but "death" within life is a mystery, even to those of us who've experienced it, a great unknown. The conscious life, the subconscious, the unconscious—such mystery. Some say our conscious dips into the unconscious realm when we dream, and the conscious mind can communicate with the unconscious during creativity. In stories the conscious famously journeys to the "un"—Jack climbs the beanstalk into the world beyond, Dorothy whirls off to Oz, Alice falls into the rabbit hole, Pinocchio descends into the whale's belly, under the sea. Literarily speaking, light is to consciousness as the sea is to unconsciousness, two classic and ubiquitous metaphors.

"But there was more," I tell the bookstore owner. "There were dreams. Well, nightmares. Lots of nightmares," I say. He looked me in the eyes. How can I tell him about the mental images and realistic feelings of death, death, and more death? Of capture and imprisonment, trickery and deceit, and hypodermic needles glinting in artificial light, dripping with toxic fluid intended to blot me out? Of nightmares that were the stuff of despicable fiction? Of nightmares that bespoke the reality of the invisible thread between the material world and the metaphysical, the natural world and the supernatural? Of nightmares that merged my mind's fiction with flesh and blood reality of people and events and smells and sounds and yes, sights, from the environment around me? How could I tell him, while we stood on gray industrial carpet next to my silver tank and his inventory of books, that I had lain in a bed with a pit dug underneath, into the earth, like Alice's rabbit hole leading to another world except instead of a Mad Hatter the hole contained an entity, an evil presence with a dark form and long claws, scraping, pulling to the edge of the hole in the earth, reaching up to me, hissing, "I'm going to kill you, I'm going to kill you . . ."

The bookstore owner asked, "Did you see angels?"

He wants to hear the report from above Jack's beanstalk and under the sea that in the world on the other side of consciousness, angels exist. I see it in his face, his eagerness, hope. And I cannot; not from personal experience anyway. I shake my head, tell him no, consider blurting out, "No angels, just demons," but I keep that to myself.

I end on a high note. "It's not like the movies," I say with a laugh. I tell him a little about the multiple stages of coma, skip all the parts about the terrors of oxygen hunger and recovery from ARDS, and focus on the rosy end. That I am glad to be alive. And thankful for your prayers. Because I am.

Being able to articulate the experience of a two-month ARDS coma is a little like being asked to describe what marriage is like. The whole thing or bits? The short version or long? The sanitized version or the one including the scary parts that might make you doubt my standing on the road to eternity and how friendly I am with God?

I finished my conversation with him, thanked him again for his prayers, bought my book and left, wondering why I felt a little deflated with a whiff of sadness and an after tone of . . . what was it? Guilt? I had been to the edge where life meets death, hovered in another world, and came home without a pretty postcard and I could not help but feel I had somehow let him down.

He only wanted to know what so many others have over the years. What's it like? Were there angels? I don't remember when, but after answering these two questions countless times, the flavor of guilt and wistfulness at wanting to give a more spiritually uplifting answer faded into doubt. No, I had not seen angels. Or a white light. No calling warmth or tunnel or any of that. The light and tunnel thing—no problem to have missed, but why in the world, why in heaven's name, did I, a flawed but devoted lover of God, get demons instead of angels? Why? What did that say about my faith? Or about me? Or did it mean anything at all? I kept these questions, these doubts, to myself.

I'd been home for a few weeks now and Tim asks me again.

"Lin, do you want to see those other pictures yet?"

No. I don't want to see them. Seeing the picture of the baby on my chest had been disturbing enough, and the millisecond glimpse I had of one picture the day he first pulled the white envelope out of his pocket had turned my stomach. Natural morbid curiosity piqued slightly was not enough to make me want to look, but there was this—he needed me to look at these.

"OK," I said.

He retrieved the envelope and set them in front of me at my desk. I looked down and stared at the first image. My body was blown up to about twice its normal size. My head was enormous. I stared at the startling sight of my eyes disappeared into swollen flesh, slits, swollen shut. My skin was gray.

It was like looking at an image of yourself in your own coffin.

I flipped to the next image and took in a deep breath, my eyes brimming with tears. I looked at him.

"I barely look human!"

"I know," he said. How does a person's head change size? How does a person experience such profound distortion and recover? I looked quickly at the other couple of pictures then handed them back to him, a whisper of a wave of suffering leaking out of him and into me, expanding into a grief shared.

"There's a video. Did I ever tell you that?" he asked.

"No. You took a video?"

"Yeah, it's short. And there's some other stuff on it. Caroline's first few days at home, I think. Stuff like that. It was taken about the same time as these pictures. Do you want to see it?"

I watched Kathy pull out the blue baby bathtub and set it up on the counter near the sink in Caroline's nursery, making sure of three things—that the water temperature passed the dab-to-the-wrist test, that the children were with her for the milestone of this baby's first bath, and that the video camera rolled.

"Allison, why don't you tell your mom what we're doing?" and Allison turned to the camera that Claire operated.

"Hi, Mom." Allison smiled and waved to her mother beyond the lens. "Well, we're about to give Caroline her first bath." Kathy worked to keep her sadness under her smile, but Claire could tell Kathy was upset. Why is she so upset? Claire wondered.

Allison continued narrating. "Mom, Caroline isn't even crying. She likes the water." Halfway through the bath Claire realized what Kathy had been dreading from the moment she'd first pulled the bathtub out from under the sink—she's missing it. She is missing it! This is what Mom had talked about, Claire thought. She looked around the room and remembered the night a little over a month ago when close to my due date, I'd sat with her and her sisters in this room, baby clothes strewn everywhere. We'd sorted and folded and talked, the conversation veering both to the future and the past. "Oh, look at these booties," we'd said. "This is going to be so cute to put on her. It'll be perfect when it gets cold. And we'll put this little baby beanie on her. She'll be adorable." Anticipation slipped into reminiscing as I'd folded tiny onesies and baby towels and told them about when they were babies, about their first baths, their first word, if they slept well when they were little, and how often they ate.

Claire hadn't thought beyond the cuteness of a baby beanie at the time, but now, from behind the video camera, documenting this first bath, the memory of my joy at what was coming and at what had been washed over her, shedding insight in its wake. Mom was training us, she was telling us what to do before we even knew we needed to know.

Caroline cooed in the water and Claire's frustration grew. She's missing it, she's going to miss it all! It was frustration of the same sort she'd felt when she was six, waiting for her ballet performance to start except Tim and I were late; she kept watching for us, tense because we weren't there and were going to miss it. And that's how she felt now. I was going to miss it. I was going to be too late.

The first time I was strong enough to dine out with friends we joined Kathy and her husband Tom for Mexican food and celebrated with raised glasses and smiles and lots of expressions of "Finally!" and "I thought we'd never be able to do this again." Then they began to talk about what we'd all just gone through with my medical crisis. I listened to Tim and Kathy talk, captivated as they shared stories of some of the more difficult moments for them, what happened on this day and at that moment, remember whens and could you believes and how it felt to them, what they'd been thinking.

Their conversation filled with emotion from the unbelievability that the four of us were actually sharing a meal together again when they'd expected the four would be three, or possibly four in body, three in mind. I listened to their shared experiences of the pain they'd been through during my two-month sleep spill out of them like a bloodletting, with an intensity and amazement that they had been through a protracted crisis with such an unlikely resolution, like a two-month-long train wreck, a near miss that left them with bruises and scars in their souls from the weathering of it, from the suffering that happens to the loved ones of the sufferer. Then somewhere between bites of cheese enchiladas and chile rellenos I realized I had hardly spoken during the meal. I'd been mesmerized listening to them but now I realized how very strange it was to listen to them tell stories that revolved around me but of which I had no knowledge. I'd listened like they had been talking about someone else. They'd been through this crisis together and had been affected, changed, bonded. I was not a part of this. I finished my cheese enchiladas in silence, feeling strangely excluded, an outsider to my own story.

March ticked by on the calendar, approaching the three-month mark of returning home, often the point after a crisis when it seems like normalcy should have returned. I had jettisoned the walker and cane, my oxygen saturation was finally staying at or above 90 during the day so I no longer needed supplemental oxygen during the day (although I needed it at night for at least two years), and at the end of the month I drove my car again for the first time since August, which terrified my children. "Mom, are you sure you can do this?" they asked as I slid behind the wheel for the first time. "Of course," I said, trying to project confidence, practicing in the subdivision side streets. I'm not sure if they were more worried I didn't have the strength to drive or if I might have forgotten how. My memory was Swiss cheese, at times frightening in its gaps and fragility. The movie *Finding Nemo* had come out this first year after my illness and Allison said one day, calling a spade a spade, "Mommy, you're just like Dory!"

It was time for the six months of meals to stop. I didn't have the strength or endurance to grocery shop so Tim did this, but if I used two hands I could lift a pot, so I began to cook some and between that and takeout and my family's help and leftovers, we managed. I couldn't carry Caroline in her infant carrier or up the stairs which meant I still depended heavily on Jacquelyn and Claire for her care, but I could diaper and feed and bathe her. Cleaning my house was out of the question, but I could load the dishwasher. I continued physical therapy. I tried to stay focused on what I could do, not on what I had lost.

My family had functioned for so long without me that they had no expectations for what my recovery and return to former roles would look like if it happened at all, but I could not say the same for myself. A mother should mother, a wife should love, a writer writes, a person must exist outside of themselves and their physical limitations. Their emotional limitations. Spiritual limitations. Every dish loaded and diaper changed was one step closer to my old life. Every day was a balance between what I could do and what I could not, between pushing and resting, trying to find where the line was between the two only to find that it was a fluid zone instead of a solid line, and some days I pushed too far and wound up in bed or tears or both. Some days I had margin physically, but my soul ached in a heaviness I could not identify, a weight over my being that I loathed, that I thought I had no right to feel because I was a miracle and I was pretty sure miracles weren't supposed to feel like this.

The heaviness squared off with self-disgust at allowing the heaviness; I wanted to feel nothing but elation at being alive, gratefulness and joy. Most of the time I did.

Every morning I awoke I sighed with relief that I was in my own bed instead of the hospital. At dinner I watched my children plop spaghetti on their plates, so thankful they were not motherless. I sat in the rocker and drank in the sweet scent of Caroline until I was nearly drunk from the intoxicatingly beautiful smell of clean baby dabbed with Johnson's baby oil and talcum. I watched Tim shave in the mornings in our bathroom again, jutting out his chin, his short downward strokes, rinsing the stubble off the razor in the stream of water, me occasionally dabbing away that spot he misses, like before, because I'm home and I'm alive. I take none of this for granted. They are ordinary moments that are no longer an unnoticed blur of activity, they are isolated moments worthy of being noticed, of taking a second or ten and really seeing them, thinking how great they are, how beautiful, how sacred even, because they are alive and I'm alive and there's spaghetti and meatballs and baby oil and shaving cream with the ones I love, little gifts of time. And that's worth noticing.

All this gratefulness and elation and heaviness took turns and I never knew which one was going to show up; I became accustomed to this even if I did not understand it. I just kept getting up, seeing which emotion vied for dominance that day and tried to figure out what in the world to do with myself. One day in March, I found myself alone in the house. I walked from the laundry room into the kitchen, paused in the den, then walked upstairs and into my bedroom. I stood at the windows looking out at the valley for a minute, then walked into my office. I sat down at my desk and ran my hands along the wood, staring out the window, thinking.

I chewed on my bottom lip and thought about each room I'd just walked through. I'd been doing a load of laundry here and there, but now I saw the unending flow of a family's clothes-cleaning and organization that needed doing. In the kitchen, there was more than a dishwasher that needed loading or a pot to lift, there were unending meals that needed to be planned and executed, tables to be dusted in the den, sheets to be changed in the bedroom, books to try to read again in the library, work to try to attempt again in the office. My home walk-through gave me an overview glance of the tasks before me that constituted resuming a life while convalescing. The stillness and quiet in the house pressed in on me.

How do I do this? I wondered. How do I go from throwing in a load of clothes here and there to getting the ongoing laundry system of a big family back in place? I need to start planning the meals again, and looking at the calendar like I used to, knowing who's doing what, and when, and with whom. I need to figure out what I'm going to do tomorrow. I need to manage. Yeah, that's it. I've got to figure out how to manage this house again, this family, and my days, my time. Where do I start? How am I going to do this?

My heart started beating faster and breaths became shallower, the heaviness crept up. I felt like I was standing in the doorway between convalescence and real living again, with responsibility as the gatekeeper. It was only later that I realized the gatekeeper wasn't responsibility, just ability.

But I couldn't think. What did I need to do first? What did I need to do tomorrow? I had no idea. Routines. I used to have routines. That's what I needed. But what should they be? What should I do first? My hands got clammy and I gritted my teeth. I sat and stared into space.

What I need is . . . I drummed my fingers on my desk, ground my teeth together again . . . what I need is . . . my mother.

The tenth anniversary of her death had come and gone while I lay sleeping. The void of her now, the realizing of the void of her, swept over me. If she were alive she'd be here. She'd come help me walk through this transition, help me figure out how to put my days back together even though I am weak and scared and altered. Suddenly I could hear her voice in my head, and I began to cry with the remembering, because sometimes when someone you love fiercely has been gone a long time, you begin to forget the sound of their voice.

She would call me up and say, "Honey, don't worry. I'll come for a few weeks, whatever you need; we'll get through this. You've been through a lot. Quit being so hard on yourself." Then she'd arrive and she'd do my laundry and tell the kids to stop putting dishes in the sink and their clothes on the floor and they should bring them to the hamper on Tuesdays and Fridays, she'd make a menu plan and a grocery list and she'd remember Windex and cotton balls, she'd organize the pantry and wash the kitchen floor taking a butter knife to the baseboards like she had before even though I insisted she needn't, and she'd reorganize my pots and pans, sorting them by size and shape with paper towels under the lids to keep the pans from being scratched. She'd do all these things like she had that time when my older girls were little and I was overwhelmed with combining running a home well with parenting well and running a business well. She'd put my home in order and tick off the plans to keep it so, making it look so easy that you start thinking you can do it and you quit thinking about how overwhelmed you are. She'd remind me that I could not do all of this, that no one expects me to, that I've been through the valley of the shadow of death and my fear and confusion and limp in walking through this doorway from illness to the other side of illness on your way to your old life is normal. Perfectly normal.

She'd walk me through this transition if she were here. Tomorrow I'll start figuring it out. Tomorrow I'll be brave and maybe ask someone for a little help, I'll get Tim to help me figure out why I CAN'T THINK. But right now, I'm going to stare out the window while the house is quiet and think about my mother, grieve her loss anew in my loss, hear her in my head with her compassion and wisdom. You've been through a lot, honey, she'd say and I would stop expecting more of myself than I was capable of doing.

At the end of March, days after I'd practiced driving again on subdivision side streets, a good friend came to town for a national radio interview, so I joined a handful of our writing and speaking friends to support her by coming to the studio during the taping and then meeting for dinner afterward. There was just one highway and a half an hour between me and the prospect of joining my friends. The idea of driving on the highway again, so fast and unsafe, far and unbound, the opposite of everything that had been my life for the past seven months, sent little currents of fear through my body. I pressed in to the currents, determined to see my friends and see if I could do this. There was a backup plan. If I got on the highway and didn't feel ready, I'd just get off at the next exit, circle back, abandon the solo trip. Tim trusted my instinct to keep stretching my recovery but was poised for a rescue if need be. I entered the highway on-ramp, got up to speed, barely, and drove past the first exit, then the next, until half an hour passed, the current slowed and I joined my friends. I felt like I had scaled a small mountain.

When the taping finished we prepared to reconvene at our friend's house. Before I left I decided to stop and say thanks to the broadcast staff. I'd been on the show several times before over the years and knew some of the staff had prayed for me. I found the producer and expressed my gratitude and asked her to pass on my appreciation to the rest of the staff and the host, but she asked if I wanted to tell him myself, that he was just around the corner. I walked into the studio and told him how much I appreciated their prayers and was ready to leave and join my friends but he motioned for me to sit down, began asking me how I was, and the chairs were in front of the microphones, then he asked if I minded if he turned them on and suddenly we were recording an impromptu broadcast.

On this first day I'd driven again, only a little over three months since I'd been wheeled out of the hospital, it was so fresh, still an almost raw experience. But there was one question he asked (which I think I answered without much hesitation), the question I'm asked often, the thing that every good interviewer always asks their subject, the question that I kept turning over in my mind on the drive from the studio to my friend's house, and from her house to home.

"Lindsey, what did you learn from this?"

I called Susan on the way home. "Hey guess what? I just drove, on the highway, and I was just on the radio."

"You what?" she said, alarmed. I told her I'd been prepared to get off the highway if I wasn't ready, but had been unprepared to be suddenly on a radio interview, and yet, it was fun and a little like putting on an old shoe, sliding into a familiar spot of comfort, me and a radio mic.

"But I'm also frustrated with myself," I said and I told her about the question.

"What'd you say?" she asked, and I told her.

"Susan, am I not doing something I'm supposed to do? I feel like I'm supposed to totally know what all of this means and be doing something because of that. What if I'm wrong, and this isn't what it means at all?"

"Lin, you don't need to feel bad about not having the answer to this nailed down yet."

I had answered the question as honestly, earnestly, as I could, but it was a limited answer. Not by design, not because I was holding back, but limited by experience and understanding and the extreme proximity from the event. I told what was true about what I had learned thus far, still in the thick of things, but the question has taken up residence in my soul, has not left me, even all these years since its first asking. What have I learned? What have I learned now? And what have I learned now? And now? I keep asking myself this from the new vantage points of passing time, I ask this of myself and I ask God. With an almost desperate need for a continuing answer, a changing answer, as fully fleshed out and nuanced, as complex and completely mined as is possible for a mind to comprehend. I've been so intent on extracting the lessons and the learning from my trauma that I've nearly drawn myself to despair at times. Am I getting enough out of this experience? Is this really what I have learned? What else have I learned? Is that enough? Is that true? What else is there? What does God want me to have gotten from this? What am I supposed to take from this experience and pass on to others, what will help them? What can I give from what I have learned?

I wonder now if the reason I've been haunted with the continual reexamination of what I've learned from my crisis stems from an intellectual and spiritual hunger to get at the meat of the thing, at wanting suffering to matter, for a reason, to maybe change as I change. I want nuance and complexity I think, but maybe that's selfish and finding meaning's not supposed to be that complicated, so I feel guilty, or less, for not being satisfied with a ready answer for myself and others about what my pain and loss has meant. And then again, when I hear others offer quick, pat answers to explain or summarize why we've suffered or what our suffering means, it makes me want to collect these platitudes and hurl them all into the air so they land like pixy sticks askew. Make sense of that, I want to say. And so I go, for years afterward, until I am weary and nearly mined to the bone from the self-examination and spiritual excavating.

There would be days to come that I would bundle up what had happened, pull at pixy sticks and bunch them into a semblance of finding my way, one, two straws at a time and offer it out—use it—for others. There would be phone calls with spouses whose loved one lay comatose, there would be stories spoken, articles written, there would be meetings in hospital waiting rooms with doctors and patients' surrogates offering input on end-of-life issues at their request, and always an ear for friends at the end of themselves. There would be offering-it-out moments with the pixy sticks still askew.

One of my early days back home, I walked into Caroline's room for a diaper or an outfit and stopped, alone in the room, taking in the room as a whole. I looked past the single diaper and saw the rose-hued tile counter filled with an array of baby supplies, the pink bottle of baby lotion, the yellow bottle of baby shampoo, and minute clippers, the pink and white ceramic figurine of a little girl on her knees praying with a key on the back to wind its music box, the teddy bear that talked when you pressed its tummy, and one newborn outfit after another hung on small hangers lined up in the closet in a tidy row. I took in all of it and suddenly felt as if I were standing in a store—everything was new to me. Except for the crib, I had not purchased any of these things for my baby, they were all gifts that had poured in over her first two months and not only had I not purchased them, I hadn't even been present when most of them were given. Maybe Jacquelyn bought some of them, maybe Claire. I just knew I had not and in this moment I saw all of it as a whole, a nursery stocked with things I did not recognize for a baby I did not know. And right then, I didn't think about being grateful for the generosity it all represented, I just stood in the middle of the room feeling like a stranger.

I remember the first purchase I made for Caroline.

"Look, honey. Mommy bought you something." I held up *Pat the Bunny*, the classic interactive board book, then sat down and pulled her into my lap and read each page. Can you pat the bunny, Caroline? Who's that pretty baby in the mirror? It's you! I kept this book in the kitchen and read it to her almost daily for months. I would hold her and pat the bunny with her, lift the tiny piece of fabric "curtain," close it and hold it in my hands, a small testament, almost as if I were trying to convince myself that this book was purchased for this baby in my lap by this baby's mother, and that mother was me.

Another memorable item I bought her was a little bigger, a piece of furniture, and it was unusual because I bought it on a whim. Well, on a compulsion really. Furniture is not something I usually have the financial wherewithal to purchase on a whim, but on this day, in that first year home, I don't remember exactly when, I found myself at Park Meadows Mall somehow lured into Pottery Barn Kids. I looked at every section of the store, dollhouses to quilts, then wandered to the back of the store and sat down in the rocking chairs, each one of them until I stopped at one, like Goldilocks who'd found the chair that was just right. My rocker at home was wooden, without seat cushions, horribly uncomfortable, scratched and looking every bit its fifteen years old and I'd never liked it when it was new. But this chair, perfectly named the Dream Rocker, with its down seat and overstuffed arms and butter yellow slipcovers, captured me. I rocked in the store, oblivious to all the shopping patrons, imagining the bedtime story-time rituals in this rocker, until I could almost feel Caroline's head against my arm and chest as I rocked. I could rock her in comfort in this. It would fill her nursery with beauty, beauty that I had chosen. It would draw us into its overstuffed-ness for our mother-baby time where I would read to her and rock and sing, night after night, this Dream Rocker, this facilitator of bonding.

I pulled out a credit card and bought it on the spot, quickly, before I could talk myself out of making such an expensive spontaneous purchase, compelled almost by an urgency to cradle her in this Dream as soon as possible, before another day passed and added to the many that stacked up between her birth and now. Perhaps in this Dream I could recapture a bit of what I'd lost, what she and I had lost, we could make up for the missing days by packing our nightly ritual with as much meaning and love as possible, like a reduction sauce, cooked down until the essence is strong and rich and satisfying. I would not feel like a stranger in this Dream.

After the chair was delivered the rocking and singing and reading commenced. And one night, rocking away, after the baby storybook and a couple of verses of "You Are My Sunshine," I looked at her small head in the crook of my arm in the near darkness. She was so beautiful, I thought, admiring her in the matter-of-fact way one admires a beautiful child one is babysitting. If persistence could reestablish the broken link between us, I was determined to keep on showing up and putting in time.

"Once upon a time . . . ," I said, stroking her wisps of hair. "There was a mommy who had a baby." She looked at me, quiet. I wasn't one to typically make up stories. I was a book mommy. "She loved her baby very much. But the mommy got sick, very sick, and couldn't be with her baby. She had to go away even though she didn't want to. The baby had to have another mommy for a little while."

Surely the first mommy had loved the baby in some sacred hidden place beneath the realm of conscious love, hidden but not gone, even though she was. Surely the mommy could find that love again.

"The second mommy loved the baby and took care of the baby like she was her own and then one day, the first mommy, the true mommy of the baby, got better. And she came back to her baby."

Caroline looked in my eyes, still, listening.

"And they lived happily ever after."

I finished the small story that had tumbled out, unplanned, ignoring that I did not feel the love but I knew it to be true nonetheless, and Caroline looked up at me, reached her small fingers out and to my shock touched my trach scar. Like she knew what I was saying, this child who could not yet speak, like something invisible and iron-strong connected us with a mysterious understanding. I knew she could not possibly comprehend what I was saying, that my storytelling and her action were coincidence, but sometimes mystery defies what our head knows and we feel God reach down into the ordinariness of nightly ritual and speak to our heart with a whisper. Our eyes were locked, her fingers touching my throat at the place on my body that bore testament of our story. I closed my eyes, mesmerized by the grace of the moment.

20

SOMETIMES WHEN A LIFE has been badly shaken, cracked even, there is no definitive moment that marks when a semblance of wholeness returns, if wholeness is even possible; rather, healing comes on gradually, imperceptibly, so there's no memory of when the healing specifically began or even where you are in the process, like a wound that has begun to scab over, without a moment where you look at the wound and say, See? Now. The scab is beginning now. Instead you wake up one day and the wound is less fierce, a thin covering of healing has begun, and you don't know when or how exactly it began.

Months after I'd come home, enough time for the scab to begin, someone, I don't remember who exactly, asked me to come speak at their church, tell this story, let their congregation who had prayed for healing see that healing had been given, no matter how completely or not. I was not dead and that was astounding. I spoke for five minutes the first time, the next time ten, as I could. I'd been speaking publicly for many years prior to this, so I was comfortable on the platform. But one day after I'd climbed back up there again the first or second time, despite my fears that I might not be able to think clearly enough to communicate any more, someone came up to talk with me after I spoke. A man walked up to me, smiled, and stuck out his hand.

"I just want to shake the hand of a miracle!" he said. There it was again, what Coletta had said to me in the hospital. I shook his hand, smiled back, and covered over with chitchat the startle his comment gave me. That God had done a miracle I had grown accustomed to hearing beginning the day I'd woken up. That I *was* a miracle was a different turn. I knew he meant that he saw me as living proof standing in front of him, that he'd prayed, God had said yes, and my healing against all odds was miraculous. Therefore it was a miracle. Therefore standing in front of him was the object of that miracle, me, therefore, I was a miracle. I understood this string of connective thinking, but I was not ready to *be* a miracle. I was fine that I'd been given one, but being one felt inappropriate. You are calling me a miracle? I thought it might smack of sacrilege because I was pretty sure miracles didn't drink margaritas. He could as easily have been calling me the pope or Madonna, the non-singing one, or an angel or a stigmata bearer, for the discomfort I felt. Later that night at home I thought about his comment again and it lodged in me, splinter-like and full of doubt. And every time I thought about it after that, which was a lot, and every time I heard this said again, which was also a lot, I struggled with finding and making an appropriate response, and wanting to take a very deep breath and stretch my shoulders from the weight. Because burdens are like that.

Much later I talked with a new acquaintance, a man who was an ethicist, a Christian working in a secular job.

"Some people call me a miracle," I said, explaining.

"You're not."

"I didn't think so."

"It wasn't a miracle."

"No?"

"No." He spoke of medicine and prayers and how they can comingle without the miraculous in his view. I listened, chewed on the ideas, and left with a tumble of relief that a person of faith was removing the miracle moniker, but also disturbed. I could imagine how poorly his explanation would go over to the sixty people who had gathered in the church basement one night as I lay near death, praying on their knees and pleading for God to intervene, or the hundreds who wrote saying they were praying with an inexplicable burden for me, friends, family, and strangers alike. He was suggesting to wipe out the moniker and the event, even the possibility of the event, in one pass of logic. I sighed and wanted to stretch my shoulders again. Wasn't there some way to understand what had happened to me that lay short of a hyperbolic pronouncement that I was something I most likely was not, without the denial of mystery?

Between giving God the credit for something and explaining away the credit with argument, no matter how reasonable sounding, I was pretty sure giving credit was the safer bet. A bet that was all wrapped up in the idea of not insulting the Almighty and the very nature of faith itself, of our beliefs in the purpose and outcome potential of prayer, a vast subject, and whether we believed in an interactive personal God or not. What was the definition of a miracle anyway? Do they happen today? Are they like biblical miracles? Do I believe in them? How do I not? Do I believe it happened to me? How do I not? I took to sighing and stretching my shoulders a lot.

For a long time I found a sweet spot in the big questions by reasoning that a God who was capable of performing a miracle was therefore capable of handling me joining the ranks of those across the centuries who wanted to consider and reason and think deeply about serious faith questions. God had the entire benefit of my doubt while I pondered my questions. My questions were a spit in the ocean. Noticeable to the spitter, but irrelevant to the ocean. Besides, everyone knows a little spit doesn't scare God.

One afternoon I sat down on the rug in front of the fireplace with Caroline and a stack of baby books. "Sweet Caroline, let's sit on this blanket and play pat-a-cake. Want to read *Pat the Bunny* with Mommy?" Was I not spiritually mature enough to handle an extravagantly supernatural story? Was there a club or secret society to which I was not privy where people lined up to receive the next dole of suffering and along with it a doozy of an experience of God's presence? What had I done to miss the doozy? I sat in front of the kitchen fireplace on the pastel baby quilt embroidered with Caroline Aileen O'Connor and pulled her onto my lap.

"Dis," she'd say, holding her orange and green and white cover of *Go, Dog. Go!* I read it to her, as my mother had to me. "Dis." She points to a different book.

"This? You want Mommy to read this one now?" I took the book from her hands. *Are You My Mother?* I'd loved this book as a child.

I put the book down. "Let's read *Go, Dog. Go!* again." Dogs seemed much safer than mothers.

In my study, I pulled out a pen and paper. I stared out the triple windows that overlook the fields and the valley beyond and the mountains beyond that and thought again, as I had so often, of the question that loomed largest. The question I had been asked on the radio at three months out and that I asked myself in some shade or another every day. What did I learn?

Well, what did I learn? What had I learned?

I picked up my RSVP pen, the one that wrote smoothly despite my still shaky old-lady-impersonating handwriting, and wrote at the top of the page: What I Learned About Living By Almost Dying. The letters were wiggly, loose and unsteady, just like me. I still found it odd that after all these months my normal handwriting had not returned. I looked at the mountains, chewed on my pen. Then I wrote.

> That loving and being loved is a breathtaking gift.
> That being fully awake is delicious.
> That prayer is incomprehensibly important.
> That our lives matter.

That community is your safety net.
That every moment counts.
To never leave anything unsaid.

My short answer, my early-release radio answer, the nut-graph answer, had been that I'd learned to live life as a gift. And I had, even though it sounds like a fatigued cliché. This list had all come out in a rush. I finished, pushed the paper back, and put the pen down on top of it, looked at what I'd just written. Like the farmer said to his pig in *Babe*, "That'll do." For now. Each item felt true to me, solid, but something was off, something that would nettle me, like a sticker lodged under your skin, invisible, but bugging you.

It's another night. Bedtime again, story time. I pulled the turquoise book off Caroline's bookshelf and snuggled her into my lap as I read the title—*Are You My Mother?* I opened the book and began reading about a mother bird who sat on her egg, but when the baby bird came out he didn't see her anywhere. Caroline pointed to the bird. I read how the baby bird wanted to go look for her, and my voice caught in my throat. I paused, then continued. He didn't know what his mother looked like. I stopped reading. Caroline looked up at me. And then I closed the book.
One cannot simultaneously read and cry.

Six months after I'd been freed like a jailbird, I finally could care for Caroline with modifications in mothering (I never once carried her in her infant seat because she outgrew it before I ever regained strength to carry her in it) and lots of help from the family, friends, and part-time nannies we hired; Becky, Rosemary, and Emery filled my gaps in the coming years. Jacquelyn was able to get a part-time job and begin planning her return, which was really her start, to college.
It was July, seven months since I'd come home from the hos-

pital, almost a year after it had happened. Tim and I decided I should go to a publishing convention in Florida; the book I had written just before the coma was now being released, *If Mama Goes South, We're All Going with Her.* Oh the irony. I had a lot of friends in the industry who would be there to help me, and my publisher was very kind and accommodating. I even agreed to speak to a gathering of booksellers one afternoon. A fabulous publicist was hired and she escorted me around the convention with the care one would give valuable but fragile goods.

Sitting in the ballroom waiting for my turn to speak, I suddenly felt my energy drain like a lithium battery that can no longer hold a charge. My editor, seated beside me, noticed, but kept her concern to herself. I took some deep breaths right before I had to go on, walked onstage, forgetting to take off my very ugly sweater beforehand, and managed to get through it, although quite inelegantly. There were moments while my mouth was moving and words were coming out, that my brain was a millisecond ahead of myself, thinking, I hope I remember what comes next. Oh yes, this. And I'd say this. Then I'd think, and what comes next? Oh this. And I'd say that, constantly fearing that the short-circuiting I felt in my brain would expose me. That I could put two sentences together after not being able to continued to shock me, and enabled me to walk up on that platform and keep standing there, uttering sentences, despite my fear of my brain failing me, again, in front of hundreds of people. No one knew that the part of my brain that had taken a hit still struggled with facial recognition and my memory was still very spotty. The lapses, of seeing someone I knew that I knew, but being unable to remember who they were, or worse, mixing people up, thinking I was talking to one person and not realizing until some error in the conversation that I was talking to someone different, were becoming far less frequent.

Tim had been in Miami working and met me in Orlando.

"How's your breathing?" he asked, one arm still around me.

"Well, funny you should ask." We laughed. "Not so good actually."

"Really? Tell me."

"This humidity is difficult. I feel like I'm trying to breathe water." His eyes widened. For the rest of the weekend he watched my breathing and need to rest so closely that I didn't have to. He'd had no qualms about me getting on a plane alone on this first trip post-insult knowing how to handle a wife with physical limitations and an adventurous spirit. I love that in a man. Hold me, release me. How does he know?

That weekend two things happened, one dealing with my body, the other with my soul, that reminded me I was on a journey of recovery, not recovered, and not yet found.

The first small moment came in a preemptive assist from a friend, not unlike what I used to do for my children when they were small. I'd watch them running around at the park, playing and sweating and wearing themselves out without realizing it and I'd take them in for naps before they hit the wall of their ability. I don't know what my friend saw in me, I just remember her walking me back to my hotel room, sitting on the edge of the bed as I climbed in, asking me for my schedule of meetings the next day, getting their names and numbers and listening to her call them. "She cannot do this," she said and she canceled my appointments.

Another friend, one of my editors, knowing I was hardly sleeping at night, had slipped some melatonin in a paper film package and brought it to my hotel room and slid it under the door. That night I slept a little and stayed in bed half the next day, aching, tearful, wondering how I was going to get myself home. I'd been pulled from the playground, shocked that I'd not only hit the wall of my ability but that I hadn't been able to anticipate it. This was a new game. You think the line is here, so you go up to that line, but what you don't know is that was yesterday's line, today's is back there and who knows where tomorrow's will be because physical recovery is not linear; the line's always moving and your greatest job is learning how to live on the functioning side of the line, how to recover when you cross it, how to live the rest of your life with limits that move.

At the time I didn't think I was hosting my own pity party, but I probably was, in the privacy of room three hundred whatever in Orlando, Florida, but it was also a grieving. My old body could do this, my new one could not and sometimes you just need to grieve that fact. Even if you've grieved it before. No, I was not in a wheelchair, not an amputee, nor blind, nor deaf, not mentally disabled; I knew I had so much for which to be thankful. But a human is capable of the most sincere awe and gratitude for their life, while also grieving over hidden loss.

Lying in that hotel bed with a wet pillow, in pain, body spent and limitations glaring like pink neon, I teetered on a seesaw of gratefulness for breath and an ache over being lost, and I tried to balance the two so as not to offend God. If I were a miracle or if I had just been given one, I did not want him to think I thought his miracle shoddy.

The second small moment came at a rooftop table. The partially covered roof of the Denver Athletic Club overlooking Glenarm Place and 14th, set with white-clothed round tables and centerpieces and buffet tables piled with fajitas, hardly seems the place for a smackeral of undoing of one's soul. And it was certainly an innocent enough exchange. Fascinating actually.

A mix of interesting publishing people milled about the rooftop talking on a beautiful early summer evening. I sat down at one of the tables and chatted with my tablemates, a novelist to my left, a nonfiction writer across the table, an editor to my right. Group conversation shifted to clusters of one on one and someone began asking me about what had happened to me. The angel question arose.

"No, I didn't see any," I said. I sipped my water.

They asked the other near-death questions I'd come to expect and I explained the no heaven, no lights, no tunnel, no angel version of near-death and coma, leaving out of course the bit about the demon-drenched dreams. Some things just don't make for pleasant dinner conversation.

"Have you heard about the book *90 Minutes in Heaven?*" this tablemate said.

"Oh sure."

"Huge sales."

"I know."

Then she told me some backstory about the book. Apparently the pastor had been speaking a good bit overseas, telling the story of seeing heaven during an hour and a half he'd been declared dead on the highway after his car was struck by an 18-wheeler.

"Dead man walking they call him," she said and described revivals he spoke at overseas with swarms of people coming to faith in God after hearing this man's story.

"Really?" And then I had nothing else to say.

So someone had been to the edge, or apparently crossed it, and came back with the pretty postcard. The significant postcard it seemed. Swarms of people and all that.

So where was heaven? I hadn't technically died so I understood missing that part, but one doctor told me I'd certainly been "circling the drain." Where had God's presence been? Why didn't I get that story? Why? I'd been convinced I hadn't wanted it but now I lost my assurance of my own tale, a very dangerous proposition indeed. I hadn't lost the veracity of it at all—truth that this indeed happened in this way, as best as I perceived and remembered—that was my professional code and the cornerstone of my personal structure. But really, however true, was this the story I wanted?

I felt a little suspect for both not having had a come-to-Jesus meeting and for expressing that I was not unpleased with that fact. That exchange stayed with me for a very long time. Well, why didn't I? Frankly I didn't care there had been no light-choir thing, but missing out on God? Missing what some have described in their near-death experiences of being surrounded by the indescribable love of God, all feeling and fireworks? Yeah, that. I missed that.

A few months later, it's somewhere between two and three a.m. again, I wake with a start, maybe even a scream. My nightclothes cling, damp with perspiration, and my heart pounds. I look around my darkened bedroom, hear Tim breathing rhythmically next to me. Of course it wasn't real. But I can still feel the cold steel in my hand and smell the acrid gun smoke.

I'd been walking through a courtyard, out double glass doors with a three- or four-story red brick building to my right and another to my left. People are casually sitting at tables and walking about their business. I walk in the center of the courtyard as if down a line dissecting its middle. I slip my hand into my coat pocket. Then I see them. Men in black trench coats and black turtlenecks, black paint on their faces, stand on the roof and they lift rifles and begin firing down on all of us. People fall, red pools, and I'm engulfed in the center of it. Then I draw my hand out of my pocket, holding gunmetal. I begin firing. First at the men on the roof, and one of them falls, doing a midair summersault like the stuntmen in the Old West show at Silver Dollar City. But I keep firing. I fire into the courtyard. People fall. Red everywhere.

I blink again and look around my bedroom, breathe deeply, then close my eyes trying to erase the horror of the warlike violence I just saw in my sleep, participated in in my mind, felt in my body. I walk into my study, flick on the light, grab a book, but I do not open it. Oh dear God. Help me. What is wrong with me? Please help me.

The nightmares continued as they had intermittently since I'd come home, mild at first, then growing more disturbing, and now this harrowing evil. Death. There always seemed to be death. Sometimes I was stalked. Sometimes those around me. Only that once had I been the stalker. But always some aspect of death was broached and it usually led up to mine. Going to bed at night became a deep dread whether I faced insomnia or somnolence—I would either sleep for three, maybe four hours, then I'd awaken and remain awake to stumble through the next day, or I would sleep and see terror. Terror by night, depression by day, for months. Please help me, God. Help me.

Fifteen months after I'd come home, I slid open the glass doors from the den one afternoon and walked out on the deck. It was an unusually warm day for Colorado in March and I looked at the mountains in the distance. Tim was at work, the children were at school, and Caroline, now almost nineteen months old, dragged her tan plastic rocking horse with the blue saddle onto the deck too, scraped it across the wood planks, to play behind me. The wind whipped my hair into my eyes and I reached up and tucked it back behind my ear with a shaking hand. Why was I shaking? I tried to stop, like I had been for days. But the tears wouldn't stop either. I let them stream down my face as I looked at the mountains. I wasn't feeling sorry for myself, I wasn't sad. Just a wreck. I had no idea why.

That night, Tim held my hand. "Look, we've got to get you some help," he said, with tenderness and the calm assurance of a man who sees things plainly, without sentimental gloss, and doesn't quake in his boots when the facts are bad. Pragmatic. Fix it. Apply logic. Make a plan, then work the plan. It was a short conversation, my man of few words and decisive actions, but I'll never forget his eyes right then, blue-green and pooled with compassion. How does he do that? How is he not sick to death of this whole business of illness and its aftermath? How does he keep bearing up? I remembered a conversation I'd had when I was in the hospital with the man who'd come in to clean my room. He'd picked up my garbage can and asked me how long I'd been in the hospital. "Months," I'd said. "That's rough. I was too," he said. "It's rough on the family too. My wife couldn't handle it. She left." I was shocked, but turns out this reaction is more common than stoicism or heroism; some sources say 75 percent of marriages among the chronically ill end in divorce.

It wasn't that Tim hadn't had his moments. One day when I was still in the multi-trauma unit at Swedish and had been awake for a few weeks, he came for his post-work daily visit and for the first time he got snappy, his square jaw clenching in the way it does when he's trying to hold something in. How many consecutive days can a man hold a pink kidney-shaped pan for his wife to barf in without wanting to barf in it himself from the tedium of endless kidney-shaped pans and months of sitting in hard plastic chairs, drinking vending machine coffee, smelling antiseptic and sickness, getting your heart yanked around from the yo-yo of bad news/good news/worse news that is life in ICU, life for the family of the critically ill. "Go home, honey," I said. "Thanks for coming today, but go home. Rest." He did.

There'd also been that day at the four-month-home mark we went out to celebrate our twentieth anniversary. The actual anniversary had fallen midweek during a work deadline of his, and on that night we ate dinner at Wendy's. Some people take European vacations to celebrate twenty years, we dined at Wendy's. Later that week at our Anniversary Redux we sipped champagne cocktails at a small table, little candle glowing, and ate crab cakes and Snapper Ponchartrain, dripping with lobster white wine butter sauce. My anniversary card for him lay on the table.

Somewhere between the I'm so glad you're not dead and the I love you, he said, "You know, when you were in the hospital you had a really bad personality."

"I what?"

"You had a bad personality."

I narrowed my eyes, tilted my head.

"I had a bad personality? What kind of charm and winsomeness were you expecting from someone with plastic tubing protruding from seven or so places, who, who . . ."

"Sorry. It's true."

"I had tried to be the easy patient, the low-maintenance patient. When I could talk again I was always asking that one nurse questions and giving her encouragement about her life, listening to her stories of her troubles with her mother and her boyfriend . . . I . . ."

"Sorry, hon. You did."

Now, on the rare occasions Tim suffers the indignities of a cold, I ask him how his personality's holding up.

21

HOME ALONE IN THE SILENT HOUSE I sat down at my
desk, stacks of books, piles of papers, notebooks comforting
me with the familiar. I had kept the piece of paper on which I'd
written my Learned About Dying list in a notebook ever since
I'd written it months before. It seems probable that I'd have read
it this day, although I cannot remember for certain, only that I
found myself lost in thought and remembering, about 107 days
in a bed, about God and his whereabouts.

Windows on two walls angled in the perfect direction to
catch the late-day sun like a funnel pouring golden light into
my study, warming my desktop to my touch and casting the
room with a soft glow. I pushed back in my chair away from the
desk that faced the fireplace, swiveled so I faced the windows,
and stared off into the middle distance between the field and
the mountains, the middle distance, that place that leads from
thought to thought until you are lost in the terra incognito of
soul contemplation.

What then, if everyone else seems to know what your story
means but you?

"What have you learned from this, Lindsey? What does your
coma, near-death, and now brain injury 'mean'?" I have no
idea! That I'm what? An ingrate? Thick? Undeserving of my

dramatic rescue? To be sure on that last one. Maybe life is just one happenstance after another—randomly.

If life is just one random event after another, then what does it all mean? Nothing? You live your life, love your people, bow to your God, and then you die and none of it means anything except you get to walk through pearly gates in the end?

Maybe this was why my What I Learned list had seemed lacking in complete authenticity and far from the whole story, missing complexity, too much like a spoonful of sugar on top, true but trite. Maybe I'd just nearly died, then suffered a lot, had gotten a gift, suffered some more in hidden places, and now I just had to be content that so many other people had found fully fleshed meaning in the story, as so many have told me.

I'm still to this day not sure how to answer people when they question me or wrestle with the contrast of my story when so many desperate others pray and get a no, or no answer. How could I question without diminishing so many others' experience of my story, their sense that they had prayed and God had heard them, personally, and answered them, personally, and my story had become their story?

Random messed with my head. Random led me to a void of meaning. And to me that was untenable. The words that Holocaust survivor Victor Frankl wrote were true: Man isn't destroyed by suffering; he's destroyed by suffering without meaning.

Maybe all there is, is the trite bow, your story means "this" or "that," what it means to everyone else, end of story, and if I fall apart now, after all this, then maybe everything that we've all endured will have been for nothing.

What if the 107 days and sleeping in the abyss and under the sea and chest tubes and trachs and tens on the pain scale, Dilaudid in the IV, breaths that leave you air hungry, missing muscles and missing love—*never makes sense*? What if some questions are too frightening to ask because what if you ask and the answers undo you?

One hundred seven days. One million and seven prayers. One miracle. And I had missed it.

I had to tell all who asked, no, no I did not see angels, or heaven, had no true tales of the palpable presence of God surrounding my hospital bed with a supernatural aura, or fascinations untold and a two-month pile of postcards from the depths of the mysterious realm of unconsciousness. I had gone there and returned with only the evidence of my life to indicate that God had come near. The irony, of course, was that for hundreds of people, that was precisely the point, my life was the evidence. As a friend told me recently when reminiscing about the first day she'd seen me after my coma, "When you walked into the Castle Cafe, it was like you had come back from the dead."

The only one who seemed to be discontent with any aspect of the story was me. And I'd told no one. Not even God. I'd taken everyone's word up to this point, they had seen a body that appeared dead for months, experienced my sudden vanishing, my two-month silence, and then they experienced an answer to their prayers. They got the miracle, I got the nightmare. I had been taking their word on it ever since and figured this was a lot like faith. You believe without seeing. They saw, I slept, then woke, then believed them. My baby had a mother again, well, mostly. And most of my days since I'd woken up, regardless of the reality of suffering, had been filled with gratitude, a thankfulness for another go-round at life that made me weep sometimes from the joy of it, that made me laugh. Who in the midst of all that joy at being alive and gratitude to God for gifts untold when so many people don't get the gift they want or the yes they pray for could dare waver? No, there was one question that lingered like a feeling, a near invisible doubt, a sliver, that I had not been able to utter even in my mind.

Maybe it was something about sitting in that sun, hands on warm wood, reflecting in a silent house, or maybe now that recovery was less all-consuming, or maybe, I sensed it was finally safe to ask the question without seeming like an ingrate. God? Where were you?

For 107 days where were you? Where were you in my unconsciousness and where were you in that hospital room when I wanted to feel your presence with fireworks and explosions of emotions and supernatural palpability? Where were you, God? I began to cry.

Some have said that not believing in God is better than believing and questioning his whereabouts, and now, in the coldness of this place, I tasted the acridity of this sentiment, felt the chill wind in my soul, and I loathed the thought, the experience, the doubt, and everything about it.

I looked out the window and realized I was not dead from the asking. I was not undone. I exhaled relief, not that I hadn't been struck down as a blasphemous ingrate, but that I had finally allowed myself to ask my thorny unutterable question.

My unutterable question had been a spit-off-a-cliff-into-the-ocean question to God all along.

I thought back to that day before my consciousness came to stay when the neurologist had held one hand and Tim had held the other and I heard them asking me to squeeze their hands and could not answer or will a response and had wondered if at that moment I might be dying. The moment was infused with the mystery of feeling death close and the thinness between this world and another. But the greatest mystery of all was that at that moment, when death breathed close and I realized it—I was not afraid. It was at once amazement and astonishment and "other," and natural, a moment that came softly, changing my view of the inevitable then and now and forever.

"Where were you, God?"

I was there, my child, I sensed him telling me, I was the peace, I was the breath, I was the comfort.

I sat in my office a little stunned, then I grabbed a pen and wrote it down, trained to contemporaneously record a good quote when you hear one.

A Scripture in Isaiah says to fear not, and that "when you pass through the waters, I will be with you."[4] I was afraid plenty of other times, but having swum through the waters, nearly passing through, I can say, yeah, that's the way it was.

The act of questioning made me want to ask a thousand more

questions, a million, for the rest of my life. Frederick Buechner wrote in *The Magnificent Defeat*, "It is not objective proof of God's existence that we want but, whether we use religious language for it or not, the experience of God's presence. That is the miracle that we are really after. And that is also, I think, the miracle that we really get."[5]

I'd been looking for God in the fireworks and the feelings, and he'd been in the comfort, and in the peace in room 4273 and in questions, in community and their sacrifices, in the transcendence, all along, hiding in plain sight.

As to finding my meaning in my story I think I know this: Life-slice events that string together to make a whole life, like a divorce or a death, dreams shattered, jobs lost, love lost or a marriage gone flat, and born babies, found jobs, found health, and new loves, don't carry just a single meaning.

We want a story. And a story is a narrative with meaning. In a narrative, this happens then that happens and so on. But in a story, this happens then that and so on and the whole thing adds up to something else. This is what gives stories power. Here's what I've found to be true: There is no single meaning. But, there is meaning. I didn't find the meaning of what happened to me, I found meaning in it.

The nightmares, insomnia, exhaustion, shaking, and difficulty thinking continued, sounds amplified between my ears and my mind so the smallest of noises were a cacophony in my head that made me tremble inside and need to flee the source of the sound. At a school event for one of our kids I stood in the crowded cafeteria after the performance, felt the crowd closing in, heard hundreds of voices, crashing cymbals attacking my brain. I began to shake. Must get out. "Hi, how are you?" I said, faux smile, not sure who I was speaking to, yet they knew me. Keep it together. "Yes, the kids were great." Smile, nod. I could barely think to converse with my heart pounding and the crowd screeching. My hands began to sweat. Must get out now.

"I'm sorry, I have to go." I jetted out of the cafeteria, slipped through the front doors into the night air and to the refuge of my car. Church had the same effect. When the music began I'd step out of our row and go stand in the foyer close enough to hear when it was over but far enough away to keep the sound assault at bay.

I filled the prescriptions for Xanax and Ativan the doctor gave me, scheduled the next appointment and test with her, and tried to keep making mac and cheese, quizzing spelling words, driving carpool, changing diapers, waiting for the babysitter to come help me, tucking clean kids into rumpled sheets, "Now I lay me down to sleep. Time for bedtime prayers." "Good night, honey, I love you. To the moon and back."

Oh God, thank you for helping me get through one more day. For giving me one more day. Now I lay me down to sleep, I pray the Lord my soul to keep. If I should die before I wake . . . oh God, help me. Thank you. Help me . . .

22

ONE OF MY DOCTORS wanted me to undergo an overnight sleep study. I was still on oxygen at night, but only a low amount. Was it enough? What else was going on? Why couldn't I sleep? Tim and I checked in to the sleep clinic one evening, after dark. He walked with me back to the fake bedroom. He'd stay to hear their spiel, get me settled, then go home. The sleep technician came in and began rubbing goop on electrodes and sticking them on my head and neck and chest, which would then be plugged in so my heart rate, respiration rate, and brain waves could be monitored all night, while I partook of a "good night's sleep." This was the second test I'd had recently. Of the more than seventy or so identified sleep disorders, they were narrowing mine down and now testing me overnight for apnea on a CPAP machine.

The powder blue silk pajamas that Tim had bought me when I was in the hospital lay on the bed, my book lay on the nightstand in this fake bedroom where I'd have a no-doubt fake night's sleep. My emotions had been erratic the last several weeks. Wildly erratic. The tech stuck an electrode on my chest and Tim quipped, "Careful, you're going to flash him."

I started laughing. And I couldn't stop. But it wasn't a pleasant, this-just-cracks-me-up kind of laugh, it was a nervous giggle, unsettling, then . . . out of control. Even while I was laughing

I could hear how odd I sounded, inappropriate. The technician held a poker face and finished the electrodes and I idled down, then we got down to business.

"This is the sleep apnea machine," the tech said, pulling out a mask that looked like a cross between The Fly and a fighter pilot. Then he demonstrated.

"We attach this to your face, adjust the straps, and then we attach it to this," he said pointing to a machine resting on a table next to the bed with a hose sticking out of it. He fit the mask on me.

"Does that feel OK?" he asked. I nodded, a little embarrassed about the laughing. Then he attached the hose and turned it on. It made a mechanical humming noise, of air swooshing through plastic tubing and I heard it first, then felt the air blowing into my nose. I burst into tears and started yanking, frantic to get the mask off.

"Turn it off, please turn it off," I said. I sat on the edge of the bed crying while Tim finished removing the mask from my face and the wide-eyed tech rushed to hit the off button. No one said anything for a minute or two. Tim rubbed my back in little circles.

I looked at the tech who obviously didn't know what to do and said, "I'm sorry . . . I was on a ventilator. And that . . ." I cried for a couple more seconds. "That just took me back."

Later that night we were able to continue the test without incident, but I felt vulnerable and ridiculous and foolish, alternately laughing and crying like a woman unhinged. A woman I didn't recognize.

Days later, I lay in a patio lounge chair on my back deck. The shaking, sense of dread, crying, insomnia, and nightmare cycle had continued. Then it hit me. I can't take care of my toddler like this. Or my other children when they come home from school. If I could just sit here until I don't feel like this anymore. Quit shaking. Avoid noise. Every sound was loud with a chalkboard screeching effect in my brain. Horsy on wood. Truck on the road. Kids coming home soon. I can't do this. I can't do this. What? Live? That's ridiculous. God, what's wrong, what's wrong?

I sat in the sun like a celluloid tuberculosis victim taking in the air at the sanatorium, and I would have sat there, hands gripping the warm metal arm rests, head leaned back, eyes closed, face to the sun, for days, for weeks if I could have, until the tuberculosis was cured.

Becky was my über-nurturing sister-friend whose children were grown; the kind of friend who not only had the time and life-space to take care of me, but one with caregiving in her DNA. She'd told me to "Come, just come and rest. Let me take care of you."

"I'm sorry," I said to Tim the afternoon he told me he thought I should go. "I'm sorry I can't do this." I knew he knew I meant "mother."

"We'll manage fine. We've had a little practice."

I had ceased to function, again, was lost, again.

I don't remember saying goodbye to my children, but of course I've blocked that out because mothers don't leave, mothers don't have spells; when comas kidnap them against their wills is one thing, but mothers don't leave of their own volition no matter how tired or used up they are. It's the unwritten code. I was breaking the code.

At Becky's I alternated between sleep and sudden awakenings in the middle of the night from another nightmare or for no reason, pulse racing, fear coursing, of what? Of what? Of nothing. Sheer panic that lived in my body, determined to find some way to leak out.

I settled in her wicker chaise on her patio, with mountains in the distance I never saw. One day for three hours I just sat and stared. I had no idea, but I'd learn later, that doing that is necessary for brain healing, which would make me feel less crazy, guilty, realizing I'd actively worked on my healing. I sat in the chaise, books stacked next to me I never read, my Bible near me, meds at the ready for when I could take the skin crawling, panic rising not another second, then I'd sleep for hours in the chaise, and wake to find I'd been covered by a blanket with a plate of salmon salad on a table next to me seemingly out of nowhere, and a glass of mint tea with an orange slice like I was in a dream. I was Elijah run off in fear and depression, sleeping, angels feeding him until he resumed his strength. I was some Camille or Penelope, a woman with "the vapahs," the one taking in the sea air if there'd been a sea, the pale, sickly one, convalescing at the sanatorium on her sun-facing chaise, blanket over knees, waiting for the tuberculosis to clear.

23

I HAVE NEVER MET a man so capable of bearing up without complaint as my husband, but the new aftermath of illness had me wondering how much he could take. What if this was the unbearable straw? I wanted to squish my infirmities into a wad and shove them in the bottom of the compactor, drag the deck chair to the garage, order Ponchartrain, dance with Tim in a room glowing with flickering beeswax candles. Laugh.

One of the hardest things about being the recipient of caregiving instead of caregiver is continuing to accept what's being offered with no strings attached, accept it graciously, guilt-free, for what it is—love without condition, that bears all things, believes all things, hopes all things, endures all things—until you are strong enough to be the offerer. But Tim was right. I needed help. We were referred to a neuropsychologist, a doctor who understood neurology, how the brain works, and the psyche and also had experience with coma patients. I took the first appointment she had.

Buck up. Pray harder. What kind of person are you? Not one given to a weakness of disposition or mind. No. You are better than this. Your children need you. Your husband needs you. You're going to put him through this after all he's been through? I don't think so. Besides . . . miracles don't act like this. Knock it off.

No matter how many questions I threw into the wind or how long I spent on my knees or how hard I tried to stand on my feet, I was powerless to stop whatever was happening.

I fingered the edge of a page sticking out of my red leather notebook in my lap, where I'd written, "My brain has become my enemy. Home reentry, decisions, severe sleep deprivation (makes skin crawl), anxiety, hard time reading, thinking fuzzy, concentration-driving, energy, light-headed, asleep but feel awake, feel like my brain is waking me up—subconsciously afraid I won't breathe, die."

What if, in a wee bit, I'm losing my mind? I want my mother.

If I should die before I wake . . .

The words were strewn all over the page with things crossed out and underlined, duplicated, messy, reflecting the confusion going on in my brain.

Something was very wrong.

Soon Tim and I walked down a narrow hallway, turned left into the doctor's office, and sat down on her couch, leather I think, to wait for her. How classic. "Shall I lie down?" I asked Tim, throwing my forearm to my forehead and leaning back a few inches in a mock theatrical pose of repose on the therapist's sofa. He laughed. I studied her diploma on the opposite wall and shook my foot vigorously, mindlessly. I was already seeing a general practice physician, a pulmonologist, a cardiologist, a rheumatologist, all whom I'd collected like dominoes since the ARDS, so what was one more ologist?

The doctor entered, pleasant but authoritative, and listened intently to me describe the ARDS/coma/anoxia/debilitation wretchedness, the gradual recovery, and my current state that tumbled out in a torrent of words. She held steady eye contact, interjected questions, and did not flinch at my tears. She also shot straight—depression, exhaustion, maybe more.

I scribbled her suggestions in my red leather notebook, saving them like precious drops of water in a canteen in the desert.

Then she held out a little hope, something I was more comfortable with—we would schedule tests.

"Let's see what's going on brain-wise," she said. Tim nodded approval. Tests meant information, and information—with its logic, explanations, its ability to launch a plan of attack and combat fear of the unknown—is power. As Joan Didion writes in *The Year of Magical Thinking*, "In time of trouble, I had been trained since childhood, read, learn, work it up, go to the literature. Information was control."[6] I clutched a tissue and nodded. "Yes, let's do this. As soon as possible," I said, trying to squelch the panic constricting my throat.

One hundred and seven days in the hospital. One hundred and seven days of trauma, now a part of who I am. Months in ICU. Months on a ventilator and feeding tube. Months of hell remembered by my body if only in glimpses in my mind. Forty-seven-plus days in a coma. Forty-seven-plus days asleep. One hundred and seven days of a war now a part of me.

Trauma embeds itself into your DNA, into the memory of your cells and places in your mind that lurk and trickle without warning, long after your body heals, like a permanent scar in your brain and bones and blood.

It's a summer day, eighteen months after my war. I'm grocery shopping, pushing a wobbly cart down aisle 14, one aisle from the end of the canned goods, somewhere between Pad Thai noodles and green chili, when it sneaks up on me like a cat in the dark. One minute I'm putting Kalamata olives in my buggy, rounding the corner for rice, intending to make it to aisle 15 for French roast coffee beans, but there will be no fresh coffee in my empty airtight crock tonight.

My heart starts beating faster as I pass the frozen garlic bread, not that garlic bread scares me. I ignore the beating. But in the time it takes to walk half an aisle, my heartbeats change from unnoticeable to slightly aware, to feeling them, feeling each beat, feel them getting faster and oddly stronger. My hands grip the red plastic on the cart handle, sweating.

Take a breath, I think.

Take a deeper breath and push away the feeling, breathe it out before it washes over you and drowns you, grabs you and won't let go. All I can do is breathe, breathe faster, deeper, trying to breathe in control and ride over the crest of this thing.

But it's too late. I can't catch my rhythm to breathe, neither deep enough nor fast enough nor controlled enough, or normal, just plain old normal, like everybody else in Safeway going about the routine, ordinary act of restocking their pantry.

Then that cat in the dark slinks by and suddenly the fear washes over me. That old enemy who acts like a lover, knowing me so deeply, so intimately, in all my vulnerable places. "I've been here before," it says. "I haven't really left. I can come out and play whenever I want," it whispers. "I was a part of you. I was and am connected to your breath." The cat swirls at my feet.

My hands shake. I can't breathe. Well, I am technically inhaling and exhaling, continuing to be alive, but I am oxygen hungry nonetheless. The old panic, one hundred and seven days, forty-seven days, kicking and screaming and clawing in my mind to breathe while my body lay immobilized, that old panic is remembered in my deepest places, and now, with my hands, shaking, sweating on the red plastic cart handle, it's secreted from its mysterious hiding place and washes over me again in aisle 14.

Get out.

I have to get out.

Away from this store, this Muzak, these people.

But I have no idea why.

Like the sound of the ocean when you're underwater, all I hear is muffled, fading clips of conversations and Barry Manilow on the store speaker, my beating heart, breaths, and my own inner dialogue.

Oh no. Conquer it. Control it, don't let it control you. Get above it. Get out. Leave now.

And I do. I walk away leaving Kalamata olives in a basket on aisle 14 and French roast beans still on the shelf.

I don't remember getting into the car, or walking out of the store for that matter. Just leaving that aisle, that moment, as quickly as possible. I don't remember taking my rescue Xanax, but I know I did. As soon as I got to the car. Because I always did when these attacks came. I carried the tiny pills in my purse, concealed like a loaded weapon, ready to fend off my assailant. I'd open my purse enough to slip my hand down and finger the bottle, checking, finding security knowing it was on the bottom left corner, ready to rescue me when I needed it.

I don't remember what I did after that. But I do remember, I'll always remember, that skin-crawling moment of unidentifiable fear with no identifiable object, an unreal, surreal fear of unknown origin and cause but with manifestations of solid reality.

What in the world is the matter with me?

Oh God. Not again. Please help me.

Breathe. Ride the wave. Ignore the cat.

You're not crazy. You're not crazy. You're not crazy.

Was it a smell? A memory? What? What triggered these sudden out-of-control moments? What'd I do? I didn't do anything. But I must have. But I was just buying food.

I try to sort out what was happening and discover why simultaneously, because if I could just think through it I could understand it, analyze it, make it stop. Logic was always my friend. And prayer. Think hard. Pray hard. My maxims. But this, this invisible, unnamed alive monster defied reason, laughed at logic, slid around my prayers, slipping through my thoughts like sand, mocking me.

I am smart. I am faithful. I am reasonable. I am not . . . crazy. God, please make this stop.

I try to find the trigger or recognize the source or the cause when I feel the aura of it sneaking up, but only faintly; not a full-blown rational thought like "Well, what in the world is bringing this on?"—it's a wispy thought, smoke in the air, some neurons seeking a trigger while most of me feels the sand slipping through my fingers, the wave washing over me, submerging me, ripping me off balance, off my feet, holding me under with a terrifying force. A force that lets me know I am not in control. Not even close.

Once while bodysurfing in southern California when I was sixteen the surf caught me just so and slammed my small body not just underwater but to the bottom, grinding me into the sand. It was a power I'd never felt before. It dragged me along the bottom and I thrashed to stand up or swim out, just get my head above water, but no amount of thrashing was fruitful until the wave finished tossing me and then released me, as if to say, "Never forget this. There is power you didn't know existed." I gulped in air, dragged myself to the beach, and lay there, covered in sand, breathing hard, with a newfound awe of the ocean. So beautiful, yet an invisible power that could take me out in an instant whether I struggled or not. That thrashing, that power over me, that desperation to swim through the murky, muffled place between me and air, that was the California ocean. That was the coma. That was this moment in the grocery store.

24

TESTING BEGAN, spread out over a few days. I was taken into a tiny room where a young woman administered the test. I looked at picture cards, put them in sequence, described the action represented, I listened to a string of words and tried to recall as many as I could, I listened to her say numerals and tried to repeat, I held them in my head and tried to say them backward, I counted and added and worked against the clock. Then I went back and repeated such things another day.

That second day the woman gave me a simple mental command. I answered. "No, try again," I heard her say. I gave another answer. "Try again," she either said or I felt. Stupid mistake, I thought. Do this already! Give this woman an answer, now think. I pushed my mind to perform, tried to work it like an athlete works her body, strained to think, organize thoughts, deduce an answer, hold that in my head and communicate the answer.

But I could not.

"I. Can't. Do this!" I slapped my hands on the desk.

The young woman looked up from the papers in her hand, startled, and looked at me. "That's OK," she said.

"I should be able to do this!" I made no effort to hide my tears or frustration, anger and disgust. "You don't understand." I looked at her, leaned in. "I used to be a journalist," I said, lowering my voice on the last word to give it the necessary weight the contrast of this former vocation and my current pathetic state required. I let it hang in the air, ballast to my pain, self-loathing. "I should be able to do this," I said with a dismissive flick of my hand at the room, the computer, her papers, and all it represented—a decline of thought, a lesser version of myself, a formerly smart woman now . . . diminished, on the downside of suffering, the windward side of loss. I said it with no pride at any former modicum of intelligence, just disdain at my current processing lack, knowing full well I could be drooling in the corner from the vantage of a wheelchair, guilt piling like so much snow against the eaves that I was not pouring forth gratitude at whatever state of being I was left with from my saving. But now I grieved the loss, the contrast, I was so . . . less.

The woman called for a break and hurried out the door closing it behind her. I bent over the table and laid my head on my arms like a schoolchild at her desk.

25

CAROLINE AND I walked into the well-baby side of my pe-
diatrician's office, a cheery place with fish swimming in a tank
and bright scuba divers and a treasure chest painted on the
wall. I signed the check-in clipboard. *Caroline O'Connor.* The
receptionist handed me another clipboard.

"Here, hon, we need you to fill this out if you don't mind."
More papers.

I sat down, lifted the pen from under the spring, and looked
at the top page. Name. *Caroline O'Connor*, I wrote. Date of
birth. *August 30th, 2002.* I can't remember if my baby was sitting on the floor, if I juggled her on my lap and the clipboard
in the other hand, if I'd brought her in a stroller. All that my
memory lets me see is the clipboard, the paper with all those
lines and boxes and questions, the receptionist's face.

August 30th, 2002. Father, *Tim O'Connor*, check. Yes I have
insurance. No my baby doesn't have . . . what is that question?
Skip. Healthy, check. Skip. Yes to this, no to that. Done. I walked
back to the counter and handed her back the clipboard and sat
back down.

"Um, Mrs. O'Connor?"

"Yes?"

"Could you come back here a minute?" I walked over to her. "You missed a couple of questions."

"Oh. I'm sorry." My heart picked up a few beats. I sat back down, foot shaking, looked for what I'd missed, scribbled something and handed it back to her. Half a minute went by.

"Mrs. O'Connor?" I walked over to her.

"You still didn't finish."

"Really? I'm sorry." I stood at the counter looking at the papers she put back in front of me, the ball of my right foot ground into the floor, my heel shaking vigorously.

"Here. And here. And here." I checked. Signed. "Ma'am? Are you OK?" I looked up at her, brows in a slight uptick, small furrows of concern on her forehead. "Do you—"

"I'm fine," I interrupted.

"—need any help?" she said.

"Thanks. No." Then I sat down. What had she seen? I only missed a couple of questions? What did she see?

A few minutes later we were called back into an exam room. A nurse practitioner came in, assessed Caroline and called it all good, handed her back to me, then sat down next to me in the straight-backed metal chairs.

"Donna, the receptionist, mentioned you might be having some trouble. Is anything wrong?"

What should I say? I wanted to blurt out, "Yeah something's wrong. I have brain damage!" Or something. I wanted to tell her that I was undergoing testing. I wanted to say, "What a week I'm having!"

"Well, I'm having a little difficulty right now," I said instead. "I'm the mom who was in a coma when she was born." I nodded my head toward my baby, playing on my lap.

"Oh that's right, we remember hearing about that."

"My oldest daughter brought her in for a long time by herself."

"What's wrong? Do you need help?" There was that help question again so I began painting the vaguest picture that mothering was no cheesecake and cherries right now. "There are community services we can connect you with," she said, beginning to describe some of them.

I listened. But it was confusing, overwhelming, attractive. She asked more questions.

Then I stopped answering. I felt a cold chill. Help could carry a price I feared. What if she thinks I'm not capable of doing my job? What if she thinks I'm unfit? I shook my foot and bounced Caroline on my knee, smoothing her dress with maternal attentiveness. Oh God, what if I've said too much? I used to be a good mother. Caroline needs that mother. Oh God—what if . . . they try to take my child away? I stopped talking immediately and thought I might throw up.

I took her handout of community agencies and thanked her, stood, Caroline smiled up at me, and we left, quickly.

What had that receptionist seen in me? What did I do? I thought I hid what I'm feeling. I buckled Caroline into her car seat and got in the driver's seat, then dialed Susan. I told her what had just happened.

"Oh my gosh. Lin!"

"I know. And there's more. I won't have the report for a while, but I found out my test results this morning," then I told her I'd just learned my doctor had diagnosed me with depression and post-traumatic stress disorder, both very common in ARDS survivors.

"Well, duh on the depression."

"And she said there are indications of . . . um, brain injury."

"Oh Lin." We both fell silent a few seconds, Caroline playing quietly in the backseat the only sound, the words heavy in the air, a pronouncement with gravitas.

"So," she said. "You have drain bamage. Who knew?"

I threw my head back and laughed hard. I could always count on her black humor to pull me from drowning in my own gravitas at the precise moment, with the split-second timing and perfect pitch of a stand-up comic who knows how to bring down the house with humor made from scraps of truth and pain.

I took Caroline home, rocked her in the Dream, both arms

around her, just rocking, together, safe in the moment. I picked up the turquoise book on the bookshelf, read the first several pages, then closed the book. Reading and crying are mutually exclusive.

We rocked, then I knew it was finally time.

26

"CAN YOU WATCH THIS YET?" Tim asked. We sat late one evening on the sofa in front of the TV.

"I'm ready now," I said and he started the video. Myself in the coffin, I think again, and this is a thousand times more painful to watch than the still pictures had been. I saw an unrecognizable image of myself. I watch Susan's hand stroke my forehead that is so huge and distorted I think it looks like a child's hand sweeping across an ogre's head. I hear her talking to Tim and I reverberate with the pain of seeing my nearly dead self and hearing Tim's voice in that moment.

When the few minutes of video were over we sat quiet. I tasted the salt from my tears and suppressed the urge to sob. "I finally get it."

"Why'd you take this, and those pictures?" I asked him.

"Because," he said, "I wanted to have them and I wanted Caroline to know someday if she ever asked, what her mother had gone through to give her life."

"I get it now," I said.

"Do you see?" he asked, the still-recent pain on his face. "See why I shot that video? There's no way to adequately describe what it was like." I sat there crying quietly, taking in the shock and contrast of me in that bed then and me on the sofa now, the loss of newborn baths, my grotesquencess, and seeing not only the sense of my mortality but looking at the anguish on Tim's side of the camera.

What must have that been like for him, for my family? I had to know everything, then I listened hard like I used to when my mother read to me as a child wondering "and then what happened" until the very end. I had to ask that last question, the question Tim had been evasive in answering, the question I'd been asking since Brent's visit when he'd told me about a decision Tim made. "Did Tim tell you what he did that night?" he'd said. So I ask again, look him square on.

"Tim, that night, the death-vigil night . . . what was Brent talking about? What did you do?"

He hesitates, again. He's not going to answer me. Again. Why won't he answer?

"What in the world did you do that night?"

"I signed a DNR."

"You . . . did . . . what?"

27

BACK IN MID-SEPTEMBER about two weeks into the coma, Friday the thirteenth came, in every sense of every way that anyone, even those not superstitious, has thought about the label given to a day of the week attached to a numerical date of the month, heavy with a sense of dread and foreboding. This day and this night exceeded its reputation. It was the precipice of my family's sorrow, my husband's crucible.

It had started with the afternoon calls on Wednesday, September 11th, from the pulmonologist that I was declining and now faced a staph infection, fever, possible pneumonia, blood clots, possibly more lung injury from the new vent regimen, and lungs that could not transfer enough oxygen into my blood despite the ventilator at the maximum setting. Then he'd gotten the call from the nurse an hour later with the information that had put the news in perspective: The bottom line—if my oxygen levels don't hold, a 101 percent setting did not exist. There was no place else to go.

The phone rang like a siren at 3:40 in the morning. Nothing good is ever on the end of the line at three a.m. He answered it in a flash.

"This is Tim." It was the pulmonologist.

"Tim, Lindsey's oxygen levels have dropped once again even at 100 percent oxygen."

"Do I need to head to the hospital right now?"

"No, we're going to change her treatment and administer a paralytic. Being paralyzed will decrease her body's need for oxygen and allow her lungs to oxygenate at a level just necessary to maintain her vital organs. Because she'll be paralyzed, all of her breathing will be controlled by the ventilator." Since Caroline's birth almost two weeks ago, my body, even though on a ventilator, had still been initiating the breathing response. Now I'd have no breathing trigger. The vent would do it all—force air into and out of my lungs.

The pulmonologist continued. "Why don't you get a couple more hours' sleep and we'll meet at the hospital sometime before six."

"OK, I'll see you then." He hung up. Get more sleep? Right.

The doctors left no room for doubt that nothing else could be done so that afternoon Tim called the friends keeping our two youngest children, asked them to bring Collin and Allison home, and in the early afternoon that Thursday he left the hospital with Jacquelyn and Claire. They walked into the house, Claire went ahead and Tim turned to Jacquelyn.

"We're going to have to prepare the rest of the kids. Would you get all of them together in the bedroom?"

His kids would not be blindsided with the news while at a neighbor's house. No, he wouldn't let that happen to his kids; he would include them, consider them in the seriousness of what they were dealing with, and prepare them for what might occur. The truth, straight up.

"Sure, Dad," Jacquelyn said.

He gave her a quick pat on the back. She straightened her shoulders and walked off to get her siblings, comfortable with the confiding and drawing from it the strength it gave for her newly acquired and premature role.

Moments later, children gathered in our bedroom, Tim sat

on the foot of the bed, the sheets and white comforter crumpled at the edge of the bed, autumn Colorado light streaming in the windows, and faced our five children. The kids looked at their father with saucer eyes, still, silent.

"Kids, look, Mom's in bad shape. Things are extremely serious, she's very sick and it looks like Mommy's not going to make it, and . . . ," he paused, "we need to prepare . . . in case that happens."

Instantaneously, grief rushed into the quiet vacuum of tension and foreboding; silence, and then . . . a communal, audible grief.

This was the first time he'd admitted to all of them what they each probably sensed in some way, but nothing can prepare a man to tell his children, or prepare his children to hear, that their mother is going to die today.

He rose from the bed and wrapped all of them in one big bear hug, father and children crying together, lingering in the hug.

"It's going to be a hard day. We're going to have to wait. But, even if she's taken at this point in our lives we're still a family. We'll continue to exist as a family. We'll remain strong as a family and life will go on. It will hurt. But life will go on. And we'll find strength and comfort in our Lord." Then holding his kids, he prayed with them, and held them a little while longer, having executed one of a father's worst duties.

At nine o'clock the next morning, Friday, September 13th, Tim and Susan reentered ICU, Claire and Jacquelyn joined them, and friends and family packed the waiting room. The hours ticked by and few moments were spent eating or sleeping or sitting. They stood at the bedside, they walked the halls aimlessly, they waited. Outside the clouds darkened and boiled, then unleashed a fury from the skies. A torrent of rain, more than an inch in half an hour, shut down Interstate 25 in both directions for a time, several cars were almost submerged, and up to a foot of water flowed near stores on Broadway, just south of the interstate, as if the elements had conspired with the dire scene inside.

I'd steadily declined all day and now they told Tim I was at 100 percent oxygen, 100 percent pressure, 100 percent chemicals. Blood pressure was dropping. So low they now had to use a radical drug they'd not ventured to use before. It effectively cut off blood circulation to arms and legs to keep circulation and pressure in the vital organs; it was like keeping just a torso alive. Tim stepped back while they worked, death vigil begun.

A little later, he sat down in the waiting room with his two oldest daughters, looked them in the eyes, and saw something they needed.

"Look, girls," he said. "If there's anything you want to say to your mom, now would be the time to say it . . . to say good-bye." He paused, let the words soak in. He wanted them to be spared one of the biggest remorses of untimely deaths: things left unsaid.

Collin did not want to face what was going on or come to the hospital much, but that night he needed to be there and he was needed. My friend Sue had brought him to the hospital, but he wouldn't get out of the car. Susan called him on Sue's cell to try to get him to come up and join the family. What does Collin need? she wondered. She thought he needed to be a part of what the family was going through, not distanced from the emotional reality. Empathy was already hard for him.

If he never saw everybody cry, if he never saw the pain of the drama unfolding for his family, if he wasn't a part of that, how was he going to be a part of what was left when I was gone? She wanted to impart a sense of duty and responsibility, and belonging, and told him he didn't have to see me, but he should come upstairs with the O'Connors, because he's an O'Connor and this is where the O'Connors are today. He tried to talk her out of it, but it was the nudge he needed. He didn't stay long, but that was OK.

Tim took Collin and Allison into the room and the visit was short. Claire watched Allison walk out of the room in tears, and when some of the adults said it was time for Allison and Collin to go home, Claire fumed. They can't go home! she thought. Are you crazy? This is the last time they're going to see their mom alive. Then it was her turn.

She walked in and sat down, alone with me and picked up my hand, which she'd seldom done, and she sobbed, also something she'd seldom done.

Then time came for her to say the last thing she wanted to say to me. "Mom, I'm going to try really hard," she said. "The kids are going to be OK." She wanted me to know it was going to be OK at home. "I'm going to finish school. I'm going to try really, really hard."

Claire's goodbye mingled with jealousy and anger.

"You don't have to deal with this. This isn't fair. You're just there and you don't have to deal with any of this. What am I supposed to do? I don't know how to deal with a dying mother and you do," she said, wishing the mom she was losing could be the one to show her how to go through it, because that's what mothers do; they show you how to do things you've never done before and they walk with you in scary places.

"You're really doing this?" An anger that she couldn't help welled up. "Fine. Go. Leave." But she stayed long enough for the swell to pass.

Then it was time for Jacquelyn's goodbye. She'd thought all evening about her dad's counsel. She decided she wasn't going to tell me she loved me. She knew I knew that, had always known that. So she leaned over and said quietly, "Mom, I'm sorry." For the tough will that had confounded me through the years, for her teen-centric angst of earlier years. Earlier that day she'd stared out the window in this room thinking, I'm about to be a woman without a mother. She thought about getting married and having children, about raising them and having lunch out and all the thousand other things that one does with a mother. Then she thought, If I'm going to have to do this life, I have the best example. She lost her mom at a young age. She was able to do it. To live a happy and fulfilled life. She will be my example. She leaned over the bed and whispered, "Thank you, Mother."

Tim stroked my hand, my arms, shocked at the cold under his fingers. Besides lying on the refrigerated blanket, my arms and legs were ice cold, blue, from the harsh blood pressure medicine called Levophed, a medication with such dire side effects and possible outcome that amongst themselves some doctors called it "Leave 'Em Dead." He thought my limbs felt like refrigerated meat. Unnatural. Mind blowing. He suffered watching me suffer, and for what, he wondered. For naught?

The critical care doctor came into the room and Tim turned to her.

"Is this drug that you're giving her considered extraordinary measures? Heroic measures?"

"Yes, it could be considered such," she said. She discussed the dose they were giving me, leaving some wiggle room, some questionability as to whether it would be considered heroic measures or not, creating the conundrum of every end-of-life decision ever grappled with: gray area.

"Would I be out of line asking for it to be discontinued?" he asked.

"No. You wouldn't."

She left and Tim stood behind the glass doors looking out. He moved back and forth between the bedside and the waiting room.

Brent, Susan, and our close friend Kevin Mackey were nearby. "I can't take it," he said to them. "She's in too much pain." Before the paralytics had immobilized me he'd seen me get agitated and the nurses have to give me more pain medicine.

"Could I talk to you guys?" he said. It was about one or two in the morning now with the end of the night coming and now they had little doubt they faced the night of the end. He knew he was pushing the limits of coherence, fatigue, and stress, and he wanted the correction of their thoughts in case his logic was foggy, he wanted the weight of their opinion so he would make no mistake. He had no room for error.

The room was dimly lit in the way hospital rooms are at night, adding the ambiance of gravity to what they felt. The sound of the ventilator reverberated around them, powerful enough to blow a hole in my lungs and fill my body with escaping air so my eye sockets and face inflated grotesquely and tiny air bubbles made my skin crunch at the touch, like Rice Krispies.

Tim spoke first, trying to articulate his thought process beginning by reiterating my present condition: completely paralyzed, comatose, hydrated by IV, nourished by nasogastric tube, the vent doing all my breathing, my nearly bottomed out blood pressure only sustained through acute medication.

"She's at 100 percent oxygen, 100 percent pressure, 100 percent chemicals. There's nothing else that can be done to save her life than is being done. There's no place else to go." He hesitated. "I don't know if we should keep doing this." He looked at my chest rising and falling rhythmically, ashen gray with the look of death, like they were keeping a corpse alive. He could scarcely watch my body endure this.

"She's in pain. She's not only struggling for life, but she's suffering, and maybe for nothing." If they were successful in keeping me alive, was it worth the fight if I was going to be a vegetable?

His struggle wasn't which end-of-life decision to make. Turning off the ventilator was not a question in this instance. Nor did he consider removing food or hydration, none of the hospital staff suggested those steps either. Should he or shouldn't he order this drug discontinued? Within the belief system of his faith and the counsel of people he trusted and the propriety of medical ethics within the facts as he knew them, would discontinuing this acute drug with the horrific side effects and grave risks be the right thing to do? Or not?

"What they're administering now, as the doctor indicated, could be described as heroic efforts; it would not be inappropriate, she said, to discontinue it. That wouldn't violate medical ethics. So," he said, "is now the time to end the battle? When is enough enough?" He looked at the three of them. "What do you think?"

Susan's hands clenched in her lap, fearful of the weight and the responsibility of being in this room now. All of them had thought about these issues to one extent or another, but now applying them was a different matter.

Brent spoke first. "Tim, I know you'd do anything. The thing you've talked about repeatedly is keeping Lindsey around as the Lindsey you know and love and married, the mother of your children. She's just a shadow; a breathing shadow, but hardly a living one. You've said that she wouldn't want to live like that, and wouldn't want it for the kids." Brent knew the concern now was the degree of damage; with the lack of oxygen to the brain, it looked like my mind was gone, and my body was well on the way.

"But," he said. "We don't know that yet. It's not that we're in principle opposed to a passive sort of euthanasia, which is to say that you allow people to go without extraordinary measures to continue their lives," he said, "but I don't think we're there yet. It's OK to have the conversation, but we don't have enough medical data yet to make this sort of decision right now."

Kevin spoke next. He and his wife Carol weren't too long out from her having carried a baby with a chromosomal disorder, Trisomy 18.

"When Samuel was in the womb," Kevin said, "they told us that he would probably not live to be born and if he was born he had about a 3 percent chance to survive to the age of two. Then they said, 'So, if you want to have a procedure to end the baby's life now you can do that and nobody would blame you for doing that.' It was Carol's decision, but I told her what my opinion on that was very clearly. God can save. God can create miracles out of things and this is an opportunity for God if he so chooses to do it. It's his opportunity for a miracle and for me to step in and take away that opportunity was not a choice for me."

Kevin turned to Tim and despite the fact that Samuel had not survived, Kevin said, "You know, Tim, if God wants to save Lindsey and bring her out of this, it will be a huge testimony to a lot of different people. If you take that away now, you're taking away that opportunity." He spoke words which seemed especially hard-won after his own hopes during his tragedy had fallen short.

Tim looked at him, nodded.

Now it was Susan's turn. While the three of them had spoken, her stomach knotted, yet she also analyzed the discussion as it unfolded, finding it fascinating, what they'd said and the great gentleness and compassion with which they'd said it.

She saw that Tim couldn't stand the idea that his wife was lying there in pain and he was responsible for the continuing efforts to keep me alive. She saw his mountain of responsibility, the weight of his sense of duty that a decision to protect or release needed to be made and could only be made by him. She saw that his driving motivation was my benefit. He wanted me out of misery more than anything, but he couldn't do it if it wasn't ethical.

Susan cleared her throat. "Tim, there's no way we can know if she's in pain or not. We do not know that she is hurting and we have every reason to believe that she is not. If it's true that there's no higher brain function now, it's very likely that she's not in pain. She's not displaying physical manifestations of that at this point. Besides, if I'm wrong and she is in pain, it's not the kind of pain she'll remember when she wakes up."

It seemed to Susan like the unconsciousness she'd experienced in surgery where you're chemically asleep and don't come out of surgery aware of trauma you endured during it. It seemed more like people in car accidents who say "I remember there was a car." She tried to shift Tim's sense of responsibility from getting me out of pain to ensuring he didn't make an ethical mistake because of his fear of my pain, and she wanted to comfort him that he had done his duty.

She continued. "However, if she is in pain and is going to

remember it and I'm wrong, if she's alive in there and functioning in there, she'd want to be alive to be with her baby." Susan felt like she was pleading for my life.

Then, like Brent, she raised questions of the extent of the medical community's knowledge thus far. "They can say at this point when we tested her she had no higher brain function, but they can't know what that means for sure for her, what it might mean tomorrow. She may be in trouble, but we don't know. We need to embrace the limbo for a little while longer."

The counsel penetrated Tim's tired mind and his thoughts began to crystallize. On one side of the equation, he thought, was a loved one who might be significantly brain damaged, and at the moment struggled for life, to just breathe, but on the other side of the equation was his belief of an afterlife as the ultimate outcome, something to be embraced, not feared, and the comfort of that realization makes it a little easier, no less painful, but a little easier to let go, and to realize that the optimal objective isn't life at all costs. Life at all costs, he thought, is not a mandate. And so, through the long vigil he wrestled with refining this belief and applying it.

Tim walked out and sat down in the waiting room and decided what to do: Nothing. Which was indeed doing something. In fact, it was the biggest decision of his life.

The drug would not be stopped.

Friday the 13th passed within a breath of death, as close as possible without crossing over, a day and a night that the family called the death vigil. Despite everything they heard and saw, Saturday, September 14th broke, because night does not last forever. Now Tim began deciphering extraordinary measures from ordinary ones. At six thirty that morning a new pulmonologist rotated onto my case. He came in for morning rounds and told Tim he'd looked at my morning X-rays and that I'd developed a pneumothorax—an accumulation of air in the chest and pleural space around the lung resulting in a collapsed lung. A hole in my lungs was not unexpected because of the intense pressure with which they were forced to ventilate. The doctor wanted Tim to authorize him to insert a chest tube, a procedure called a chest tube thoracostomy, where he would place a hollow plastic tube between my ribs into the chest to drain the trapped air, allowing the lung to re-inflate and the hole to heal.

"Dr. Fenton, is this in any way considered a heroic effort?" Tim asked. I was beat up, and still hovered near death, and after last night he could not bear the thought of more trauma inflicted on my body.

Doctor Fenton immediately replied, "Absolutely not. Chest tubes are done quite frequently. It can be done in her room without the need for any more anesthesia because she's still in the drug-induced coma."

Tim took the pen, grimaced, and signed off on the chest tube insertion, an ordinary measure, even though they were cutting another hole in me.

After acquiescing to matching drains on each side of my chest, with the remnant of the previous night's horrific decision still lingering on him like stale cigarette smoke, he discovered the next day my status was "extremely critical."

"Any further decline," the nurse said, "cannot be countered by any method of treatment; she'll either begin to improve, or not."

Now he did something he didn't know he was capable of. She's dying, he thought. I can keep holding on or let her go. And she's not "here."

He signed a DNR, an order stating "Do Not Resuscitate."

For a day, maybe two, he agonized. Had he just killed me? Should he keep the order or not?

"Tim," Brent said, "keep your fingerprints off this."

Feeling shades of a criminal erasing his trace, Tim rescinded the order.

But what led him to instate the order in the first place had not changed. Should he change his mind again?

He signed another DNR.

And then he wavered again. Is this the right choice? He had to be sure.

For a second time, he rescinded the DNR.

The first time he tells me the story I'm dumbfounded. I'm not even sure if I was able to respond. How is a person supposed to respond to the hard truth that someone has signed a document allowing you to die, someone who would give their life for you? That both could be true was a mind-blowing, diametric opposition of an idea. How could he have done that? Yet, how could he have not? My mind spun with shock and incredulity that two slivers of space between those decisions could have been the end of me at the hand of him, or maybe not, maybe it could have been the end of me at the mercy of him. I joked, "I'm sure glad you were indecisive"; mostly I was staggered at the weight of his pain that had thrown him into those tortuous decisions and to this day I ache for what he went through.

I agreed with what he did. Or did I? I realized I didn't know what I believed about this. So, I gathered a mountain of books on end-of-life decisions and read every day for the next two weeks trying to figure out what I thought. Then I threw a little field reporting into the mix; I flew to California to interview Dr. Scott Rae, the author of ten ethics books (including *Moral Choices: An Introduction to Ethics*), and interviewed other ethicists too.

After wrestling hard with the ideas I came away believing that when Tim enacted the DNRs he was on moral and ethical terra-firma and his actions were consistent with his faith. Every medical fact indicated he could suspend life support on the right side of medical ethics; all signs indicated I was in an irreversible downward spiral toward death with no hope for recovery; he determined to keep his emotions separate from what he thought I would want; his motivation was his knowledge of my desires in this scenario. I thought Tim did the right thing, in the right way, to the best of his ability, and for the right reasons. I also learned about the complexity of the endless scenarios and variables of end-of-life issues. Like lots of things in life, the more you learn, the more you realize how much you don't know.

A month after Friday the 13th and the DNRs, two days before I would awaken, Tim prepared for the transfer to the other hospital as soon as I was stable. It was mid-October. "Craig Hospital," he'd written in an update, "is a nationally renowned facility for treatment of spinal cord and brain injuries. They have been written up in the *US News and World Report* as rating in the top ten hospitals for this specialty for the last thirteen consecutive years." At 1:00 that afternoon the Craig nurse arrived to evaluate me for preadmittance.

She reviewed my chart, including that the MRI that morning had shown no evidence of hemorrhage, swelling, or dead tissue, but Tim knew that it could not show brain impairment resulting from oxygen deprivation, anoxia. That was as much a concern now as it had been from the beginning. She picked up my hand and wrapped it around hers. "Can you squeeze my fingers?" she asked. No response.

Then she began orienting Tim on what to expect over the next phase of the rehabilitation at Craig, including occupational therapy.

"What's occupational therapy?" he asked, thinking it was some form of physical therapy.

"Well, you know, relearning how to dress yourself. Relearning how to do personal hygiene."

Tim's eyes widened and his mouth fell open as he looked at the nurse, taking in what she'd just said. Wow, that's stuff you teach a toddler. Stuff we do daily without a thought.

"What are goals? What do we look forward to as good things?" he asked.

"Well, hopefully she'll be able to dress herself in six months." The news hit him like a slap. He rolled his eyes, then questioned her about the certainty of my need for it and told the nurse he thought he'd seen a sense of recognition in my eyes in my pre-aware state, to which she replied, "Recognition does not correlate into functionality."

Then she emphasized that the two main components of the next phase were time and hope. One Tim had plenty of, the other, none, and he guarded his stoicism like a gladiator.

The evaluation ended, the nurse left, and Tim sat alone with me in the wake of the Craig nurse's words. "Recognition does not correlate into functionality." "She may be able to dress herself in six months." "Occupational therapy." "Anoxia." He looked at the vacuum suction machine connected to the chest tube entering the right side of my chest, like I was an attachment to a Hoover. Tim had grown almost as accustomed as the pulmonology team to this; it was minor . . . now. He stroked the back of my hand and arm. There'd never been a moment actually that he hadn't been concerned about a brain injury, but when breathing had become the primary battle, the brain had taken a backseat, and now, the reality was grimmer than he'd imagined.

He'd been consumed with the daily, hourly, and minute-by-minute concerns that is life lived in the corridors and waiting room and patient room of an intensive care unit, leaving him little time to ponder the what-might-bes. On the one day that he had allowed himself to, on Friday the 13th, he'd gotten the nurse's call to hurry back, he'd run into the building wondering if I'd be dead when he got up there. Now, he had to face the demon of his nightmares, pondering what his life might be like as a single father of five and the idea that my mind was dead, at least the mind he'd always known, the mind that had made me "me."

How was he going to deal with a brain-injured wife? He couldn't even imagine the radical change to the family dynamic of bringing home a person who might not be able to dress herself when I used to help him run the household, when I used to . . . "used to" was such a stark, appalling turn he couldn't even finish the thought. I might live but I'd be lost forever.

Oh this could be hard, he thought in a sweeping understatement as he stroked my hair. Now I'm going to have six children.

For the past month and a half that he'd longed for the restoration of his family, he had steadied himself on whatever daily reality was at hand, allowing his mind neither images nor ideas of an outcome that was excessively good or dire. But now he did. He allowed his mind to venture into the shaky realm of unsure emotions.

He pictured me coming home as I'd walked in to the hospital, whole and vibrant in the life I'd left on August 30th, at my desk writing, at the stove cooking tortilla soup, rocking our baby and doling out Band-Aids, dishing out counsel to our kids, and Friday night dates with Glenn Frey and Don Henley cranking from the Range Rover speakers and salty Borderitas and the anticipation of touch. And then, there remained the distinct possibility of the other end of what could be, how bad it could be, a life of wheelchairs and drool, a shell of the woman he'd married and loved, staring at him with hollow recognition.

Of the two possibilities, the first scenario would require hope and the other image tempted despair, and he could abide neither. If he allowed himself hope and it proved false because he'd expected a healing, a miracle that did not come, he feared he'd be lost in spirit and soul, his faith mangled, and his family would suffer. He had to make sure his family would survive even if I did not.

Several hours passed. He stood up and walked over to the bulletin board next to the glass doors and looked at the two pictures he'd hung—one taken hours before the birth, and one moments after. He looked at the smile he knew so well.

A gritty resolve bubbled up, a strength from a depth he'd never known, from God, as real as the unseen wind that shakes autumn leaves loose every fall. It took him back to his belief and life motto which had been tested near to the breaking point, shaken, but not broken, and had gotten him through these darkest of days.

You play the hand you're dealt.

You play it without false hope or despair, without comparing other people's hand, or questioning why you've got this hand, you just play it, as best you can, today, and the next day, and the day after that. If he could trust God to be good in a world that was not, if the end of this life is the beginning of another, and beliefs he held sacred in a God he held sacred could inform his decisions and withstand his worst moments, then he could play the hand he was dealt.

Which took him back to the words he'd written when my death was imminent. "It is my desire to let all of you know, that whether Lindsey comes home, or goes Home, glory to God."

He turned his back to the pictures on the bulletin board, away from what he most longed for, away from the expectations of how I might be, away from the images of what, who, I'd been, and walked to my bedside, kissing me as he often did, the me I was now, ready to keep playing his hand.

28

NOW IT WAS MY TURN to play the hand I was dealt. After the nightmares and panic attacks, the "vapahs" in the chaise while waiting for the tuberculosis to clear and the neuropsyche testing its dreaded news, I was the one to suck it up, to play the hand I was dealt.

The dining room of TGI Friday's is nearly empty at mid-afternoon. I slide into a green faux-leather and wood-toned booth and watch rain hitting the window next to me, drop after drop sliding down the glass, and feel cocooned in the wood and leather, a million miles away, as if I were in a pub in County Cork or London. The waitress brings me coffee and I hunch over it in stock-taking abjection.

OK, I'm still not asking "why God" questions, my gratitude for love and life stands. One check in the plus side, and yet . . . Couldn't one want to kiss the stars at the thankfulness of still living, at not having terminal anything, at not drooling in the corner, at not begging for crumbs in Calcutta or sleeping on the cold, hard dirt of a Nairobi garbage dump ghetto, at not . . . well, just read the news or live in community because everybody has . . . something. Can't we kiss the stars and still hurt?

I was a woman who had been a healthy wife and good mother before Tim lost me and I lost Caroline. Who had had babies

I'd bonded with four-fifths of the time. I was immensely grateful she was not motherless and glad I had her, though I felt it somewhat disadvantageous that she had me. But as my mother used to say, it is what it is.

I was a woman who had had a career, direction, and most important—purpose.

I don't even know now who I am.

I lean my forehead against the cool window, the sound of rain on glass millimeters away.

So. I have PTSD, post-traumatic stress disorder. Really? Isn't that something soldiers get? From battlefields. War.

Oh, I'd read the ARDS website articles about my lung-trashing injury—acute respiratory distress syndrome—with fascination and a sense of the macabre when I'd seen the ongoing memoriam section for those who had not survived, while I still wore bandages over healing chest tube wounds, like someone who narrowly misses a car wreck and cannot help but look back at the fatality behind them. I'd read the fellow ARDS survivors telling their stories and saw repeatedly the post-ARDS symptom of PTSD. I dodged that bullet, I had thought, no PTSD for me. But now, fifteen months later here I sit at this TGI Friday's booth with my own post-trauma mess.

In my notebook I write, *I've been diagnosed with post-traumatic stress disorder, depression, a coma-related sleep disorder, sleep apnea, and . . . anoxia. "Yes, your brain was hurt some," Dr. Powers had just said.*

"Highly functional, minimal brain loss." I think about those words for a moment. Highly functional . . . alright, minimal . . . that's good, brain loss . . . brain loss, brain . . .

I tally my near four months in the hospital: massive blood loss, DIC, multi-organ failure, multiple life-threatening complications, ARDS, respiratory failure, blood clots, seven chest tubes, multiple infections including sepsis, kidney failure, and two months of coma, complete deconditioning. This sum makes my heart race.

I pull a book out of my purse, lay it on the table, and examine the cover with green lettering—*Brainlash*. The subtitle seemed to mock me. I read it two, three, four times. *Maximize Your Recovery from Mild Brain Injury*. Even now, years later, when I think about this book I see those words in huge letters, taking up the bulk of the cover and was surprised when I looked at it again to see the subtitle letters are actually quite small. The author was a doctor who'd crashed while rollerblading, which whiplashed her brain against her skull causing what's known as an MTBI, mild traumatic brain injury. The book had stayed shut since my doctor had given it to me weeks ago. I hadn't needed it, I just had a mild case of depression, a sleep disorder, and a throttling case of PTSD, all recoverable no matter how miserable at the moment.

Tim had said it though in the first days of my awakening. "They said you had anoxia, injury to the brain from oxygen deprivation . . . you lost so much blood," he'd said, but the words fell like water onto a nearly saturated sponge. ". . . Twenty units of blood and blood products in one night. And your brain scans—not good," he'd said.

I sip my coffee dumbfounded at the memory of being told of a neurologist's words early on: "No indications of upper level brain activity," he'd said, which had of course been one of the salient points that had made Tim's death night vigil decision so colluded. I sit there remembering what Kathy and my friend Denise had told me about the two weeks in late October, after my awakening day, when I'd gone back into the coma.

Kathy had stopped at the nurses' desk as usual to ask how I was. She'd turned her head from the nurse and looked through the glass into my room. She saw my fingers curved inward and my arms moving up and down rhythmically, repeatedly. She turned back to the nurse.

"Do you guys have her doing that, on a machine for her circulation, or is she doing that on her own?"

"Well, she's doing that on her own."

Kathy winced and walked the few steps into the room. She saw my blank face, curled fingers, arms drawing up close to my mouth, then out, over and over, arms swimming through air.

212

Denise had seen it too. She'd walked into my room and saw me trying to talk to Tim, trying, "bwahhh . . ." she'd heard, and thought, Wow, she's profoundly retarded.

She'd also later tell me this: "I saw a depth of something, I don't know what it was, between you and Tim. There was something happening there that I didn't need to be there for. It was like you were reaching hard for him and he was trying really hard to catch you."

The warmth of a hundred summer days.

Reach hard, he'll catch me. That's exactly how it was.

Perhaps I don't remember the posturing because of the depth of coma or medication, or the inclination to bury into our subconscious memories that hold irreconcilable images of the self and if remembered they might unravel us, a tapestry thinned. But this, the reaching hard for Tim and knowing he was trying hard to catch me, the gulf between those two I will never forget.

Years later when I finally "go to the literature" and research the facts, I read, "The arms are bent in toward the body . . . the wrists and fingers are bent and held on the chest. This type of posturing is a sign of severe damage in the brain." I'm stopped cold. This was a notion I'd wiped away like dust. "Brain injury," the neuropsychologist had said. Play the hand you're dealt. I open the book and begin reading.

"Mild traumatic brain injury is an outwardly invisible illness. . . . A diagnostically subtle injury. . . . Add to that the additional category of metabolic brain injury (anoxia, or lack of oxygen to the brain), which may occur in tandem with trauma, and the plot merely thickens again . . . the loss of oxygen to certain 'less critical' parts of my brain due to heavy blood loss."[7] I grip the pen and underline the passage, circle the word *anoxia* and write an exclamation mark.

In the section about the "public mask" that can occur with an MTBI and "the elaborate plans to stockpile energy for public appearances" and the sequestering as energy falters, I draw a huge star. "With this much effort applied to performing in public, it is no wonder brain injury can remain invisible." Oh yes! "Because I wasn't a vegetable—because it wasn't catastrophic—because with my loss of brain power I still scored above average on the tests—"

Underline. Star. Two large exclamation points. *This takes my breath away!* I write and then furiously underline the symptoms she lists. " . . . don't recognize people, can't remember names, can't problem-solve, cry at the drop of a hat, sex doesn't seem to work somehow, oversensitive to everything, become easily confused, lists and sticky notes become my daily life-saver, become confused in traffic, doubt my unimpaired intellect too."

The words grab me like someone had ripped them from my brain and put them in this book. I scribble another note in the margin. *To that I add . . . one doctor says "you're getting older."—Yeah a whopping 18 months older. Others say—"I do that. We're over forty you know." Know—You don't know! This wasn't how I processed before this!*

Later I'll see I'd unintentionally illustrated this point, writing "*Know—*" instead of "*No—*".

"I wasn't badly impaired. My impairment is known as 'highly functional minimal loss.' On the grand scale, I still had more marbles in my bag than most unimpaired folks, which is nice, I suppose. But it doesn't account for my loss. Discounts my loss, actually. I'm somewhere on the Bell curve outside the sympathy line."

"Yes," I write.

"But *I* notice the loss. No, I *live* with the loss. I used to be smarter. I used to be a doctor. Now I'm a low-spark doctor. And I remember who I used to be and how I performed. There is devastating loss here for me."

I draw a one-inch star and an exclamation point with a circle at the bottom.

I grip my pen hard and look up, not hearing the restaurant's din. My foot shakes again.

Oh God. I have a mild traumatic brain injury.

One hundred seven days.

A healing against all odds, and now I am breaking apart, or nearly, or something.

Working through the thorny search to make sense of what my story meant and venturing to ask God my spit-in-the-wind questions should have been enough shouldn't it? But if I don't get my act together, what will happen to my kids? What if this rattles my marriage, strains my Rock of Gibraltar with the inch past the point he can endure and this is the malady that tops out the "in sickness" with too little "and in health" because how . . . could one man . . . endure so much? If I'm never able to fully love and bond with Caroline . . . I can't even complete the thought.

My career will probably never recover, but that's paltry to this. I remember who I used to be, but who am I now? To have been lost then, nearly undid us all, but I'd been found. To be lost now, after everything . . . I am a self gone missing. What if this shreds my soul?

I sit in my paneled sequestrator of the booth, fingers around my mug of coffee, and scream at myself in my head: GET OVER YOURSELF! Enough already! All that God did for you and now you're in a heap? All that all those people did for you . . . for what? You are a waste of a healing. Go take care of your family. Take care of your husband. Take an aspirin and knock it off. You are ridiculous! You . . . I seethed to myself.

I pull my cell phone out of my purse and dial Tim.

"Honey," I say. "I feel like I'm about to have what my mother's era called a nervous breakdown."

"About to? Hon, you're there," he says and I love him for saying what's true without a trace of the last inch.

There'd been that weekend when I'd been selected to the Poynter Institute for Media Studies seminar on "Reporting End of Life Issues." We'd sat around a large conference table telling our stories and why we'd come and views on withdrawing life support. I told mine, told of Tim's decision to sign two DNRs as I "circled the drain" and rescind them to find me again. One reporter said, "I thought I knew where I stood but now, after hearing your story, I'm not so sure."

"It makes you think doesn't it, the complexity of it all? There are no simple answers," I said and we smiled, nodding in agreement.

But what I remember most is that night. At the end of the first day after we'd left the conference table I went upstairs to my room and tossed my notebook on the bed. I was a journalist among journalists, in my element, but I turned on my computer, stomach tight, and looked at my website. I was a dichotomy, pixilated for my colleagues and the public to see—a poster-child against euthanasia and "pulling the plug," because you just never know, and I was also conflicted about end-of-life issues and their vast complexity; I was doing what I thought was expected from my story; and I was a journalist doing what I loved. Was I betraying my story if I returned to doing what I'd done and who I'd been a long time ago, a mainstream journalist who happens to love God fiercely? I took down the website and lay back on the bed staring at the ceiling, feeling my heart beating, not knowing how to be the dichotomy, not knowing who I was.

I sit in the green booth for hours, leaning into the headwind of knowing that I'm not OK, that I was lost then and I am lost now. I can kiss the stars but I have no clue how to find a self gone missing! I roll my pen between my fingers, close my notebook, and weep in time to the rain.

And then I remember a paper unread, a question unasked, and a tiny girl, waiting. I push back my last cup of cheap coffee, now frigid, shove my stuff in my bag, throw some bills on the table, and walk out into the late afternoon mist.

29

THE TESTING RESULTS lay on my desk and I forced myself
to pick it up and face it. Ink that I'd pushed away long enough.

I took the sleep study report out of the envelope and began
reading. I had apnea (thirty-four times an hour) and brain awakenings (nine times an hour) and insomnia from the anoxia. Tests
showed no stage three, four, or REM sleep! Dr. Powers said,
"You basically haven't slept in a year and a half," and my friend
Martha said, "It's a wonder you haven't murdered someone."

Then I picked up the neuropsychological report, my mouth
was dry, my throat constricted.

"Neurological consults have diagnosed Lindsey with hypoxic
encephalopathy. She continues to experience problems with her
cognitive abilities and emotional stability. She continues to experience severe sleep disturbances, panic attacks, depression and
PTSD. She was reported to have had altered mental status with
an MRI . . . indicative of an encephalopathic process . . . August
30th, [she] was thought to sustain a hypoxic brain injury."

"Eyes open, looking around the room without making eye
contact," it said, "bilateral and symmetrical upper extremity
flexion on movements at the elbow, intermittently," it said,
medical wording for the posturing, the purposeless swimming-
through-air repetitive arm movements I'd made.

Shocked, I read of an abnormal EEG at Swedish—after I'd been moved, *after* my awakening. It also said I'd only followed gestures one-third of the time, didn't follow verbal commands, inconsistently nodded yes/no appropriately, and was unable to cooperate for a sensory exam with head turning or shoulder shrug, and he "felt she had multiple neurologic issues and did not think [she] had good comprehension." This exam had taken place on October 15th, awakening day, a day I vividly remember, the day of my "what a week I'm having" look.

I shoved the report back in the manila folder and pushed it onto the back of my desk. It was evil, so I piled books on top until it was out of sight. I felt like I was going to vomit.

I sat for a long time. Well, I thought, I still have a lot of marbles in my bag, but I needed help. Mostly I needed time.

Healing was going to be a long time coming. Reading had gotten easier so I propped myself up in bed with pillows and surrounded myself in a sea of books. I canceled anything I could, scheduled recommended medical and therapeutic appointments, and started crafting a plan. I reread my notes after one of those appointments: "Realize this is common a year and a half later because things aren't the same. Get sleep and depression under control. Don't assume I can do it now like before. Modify schedule and expectations. Self pace. Relax. Try to enjoy myself. Have some successes. Write notes. Take care of my special needs. Don't be defenseless. It's a process, one stroke at a time."

I disconnected from the phone, answering machine, decisions, mail, TV, took myself off the road. I stacked plastic blocks with Caroline and read *Pat the Bunny* seventeen-ish more times, and I gave myself permission to rest as much as I needed and allow my brain to heal. Bone china, once broken, is broken, but a brain, a beautiful, mystifying, glorious brain, can change and improve and get better over time. Why is it we are often the last ones to see that if we want to take care of others, this permission to do whatever it takes to take care of ourselves is not optional?

Sometimes physical effort, even when terribly challenging,

is easier than that of the heart and mind. The first time I tried to report and write a magazine article after my illness, it took exponentially longer than I'd ever worked in my life and was so difficult that I didn't think I was capable or ever would be. I repeatedly nearly quit. Pushing through what we think we can't do depends upon our mindset. I tried to find new ways to do what I did before and wanted to do now, and worked to accept what can't be undone, and even today when I'm frustrated by limitations and after-effects of trauma, I have to remember to give myself grace. What doesn't kill you makes you stronger, they say, even if it's a zigzaggy path. Some of the hardest work we do is making the conscious decision to play the hand we're dealt.

30

A FEW MONTHS LATER Jacquelyn and I went to town for a while, shopping or some other uninspiring but necessary errand, and we headed home on the frontage road along I-25, the last few miles before our country road. How can you possibly know when you wake up on a sunny day, with its appearances of any other sunny day, shop with your daughter and idly toss a few bags into the backseat of your Yukon, then slam the door with smiles and laughs and hit 60 mph, 65 when you're not paying attention, just driving home from the store, that your heart is about to stop? Be changed forever?

My cell rang and I grabbed it from the center console. "Hello?" I said and heard my son's voice. It only took seconds for the news. "Is she moving?" I said. "Is she breathing?"

Jacquelyn looked at me, eyes wide, fear on her face. "What's wrong?" she said.

"I'm on my way," I told him, clicking "end" on my phone while I pressed my accelerator almost to the floor and handed Jacquelyn the phone.

"Call 911. Caroline's fallen out the window."

"Of where?" she asked, panic rising. "What window?"

"Her bedroom."

"Oh Mom!"

Her bedroom was on the second floor over a full walk-out basement. My little girl had just fallen three stories.

In my Yukon, flying down the frontage road, Jacquelyn gave the 911 dispatcher the sketchy information we knew and the location of Caroline's window.

"They're going to keep me on the phone, Mom," she said. I nodded. Eighty miles an hour. Ninety. Ninety-five. My chest pounded and I began to shake. For a second I thought I might lose control of the car. I forced myself to focus. What good would it do Caroline if I killed us on the way to her? I gripped the steering wheel, backed off the accelerator a tad, and willed myself not to shake, to keep the Yukon on the road. I knew I would beat the ambulance to our house.

I turned onto the two-lane road, up a hilly incline. What would I find? I knew the possibility was real that I would arrive home and find my daughter dead. Bad things, unthinkable things, happen. This much we knew.

I raced the interminable final mile, glanced at the buffalo grazing calmly behind a three-rail wooden fence as I passed and thought, What if she died and everything had been for nothing. What if after all that suffering and all that sacrifice of so many, my second chance was rendered moot by a death, a second and permanent separation without hope for my mother's heart to fully bond to my child?

There'd been that day I'd sat at the counter at Crowfoot Coffee contemplating my struggle to mother with an engaged heart and had asked myself a loathsome question about having had a baby that "good" mothers, "properly bonded" mothers, aren't supposed to ask: what have I done? But the suffocating guilt had eased over time; I'd learned I was far from the only mother on the planet who for various reasons struggles to fully attach to their child, and even so, one can still be a "good" mother. Great even.

I'd regretfully acclimated to this last bit of loss, because it was mine alone, affecting no one else, I could still love my child with all of my actions and most of my heart for the rest of my life, and ignore the part of my heart remaining closed to her as much as I wanted to fling it open, because as hard as I tried I could not make myself feel what I did not feel.

Maybe the little piece of me that could not close the final gap between us was the extra heart piece that Jacquelyn now had, forged from day one of Caroline's birth, and day two, and day three and day 107 and the months after that. Maybe instead of love multiplied by all the people loving a child, there's only so much, a set quantity, and part of Caroline's allotment had grown in Jacquelyn's heart by necessity and sacrifice and choice, leaving a tiny desiccated space in mine and that's just the way it was. It is what it is.

I would either get over it and live with the unseen guilt shards, loving her with most of me—or I'd never get over it and always ache to love more, forever; Jacquelyn and Claire would love her with more than their sisterly share, Caroline would grow up feeling an abundance of love and hopefully never know the difference. This is what I had accepted for two years.

But now—if she dies or is brain damaged—this acceptance would never have been enough. If I lose her again, like this, I could not live with myself. If she dies I'd find meaning in her death because there is meaning in her life, but if this happens and I haven't fully loved her, there would be no finding meaning in my suffering and loss.

My friend Denise once said when we do or experience something significant in life people want to know our "Gandhi" moment, our big life-changing takeaway, and if we can't find it we can go nuts. Speeding down my street now I veer my car around the last curve and feel my desperation to find my Gandhi moment disintegrate, dust under my wheels.

Only one thing matters now. I want this baby girl more than anything in my life. I want to love this girl, fully, more than anything in my life. And in an instant, I realize I do.

I want to be her mother more than anything. No matter what I find when I get there, I am. I'm hers and she's mine. And it has all been worth it. Every painful labored breath, every prayer, every effort and sacrifice made to keep me alive, this baby girl's mother alive, this family together, has been worth it. Whether it's for the rest of my natural life or just for two years. The arid heart-niches of detachment now flood like a rain over a wildfire, sudden and unexpected and welcome, drenching scorched places.

The back of an ambulance, our crying child, an EMT working to put an IV in tiny veins. Waiting doctors and nurses line both sides of the ER corridor as we come in, eleven of them, maybe less, but far too many, which I quickly count in one of those flash of a few seconds that feels like an hour. Tim and I watch as the doctors work on her. "Second story fall, OR ready," was written on a whiteboard on the wall, or maybe someone just said it. No, I think. She fell three stories. Her second-floor bedroom is over a walk-out basement. The attending physician motions me toward her head telling me to touch her and talk to her to calm her while they work. In those minutes that feel like an age we pray, hope, try to steel ourselves for the worse. Finally, the attending physician says, "I'm having a hard time finding anything wrong with her." Tension in the room drains like a mass exhale.

After an overnight stay in pediatric ICU we take her home, bruised, shaken, but whole. She had fallen twenty-five feet—one of the emergency crew measured it; a staggering distance to fall and survive. That afternoon I stand in Caroline's bedroom at the window; it's just after noon and had been a long night.

Caroline and I now look down from her window at just how far twenty-five feet is. My stomach does small flips and I feel nauseous. I put my arm around her tiny shoulders and we look together silently for a moment. She looks deeply contemplative, pensive, and I can see a replay going on behind her eyes. Her tiny wooden chair had been scooted up next to the window. On the ground lie her Winnie the Pooh lamp, shattered, and her window screen. We'd learned apparently someone who'd helped clean that day had raised her window to air out the room from overly strong cleaners and hadn't closed it. I lock it.

"Caroline, did you scoot this chair over here?"

She nods.

"Did you climb up on it?"

"Uh-huh."

"And then you fell out?"

"Yes."

"Do you remember falling?"

She nods, her eyebrows scrunched, a look of remembering trauma on her face, and she looks down.

"Honey, why? What were you doing on the chair at the window?"

She looks at me. Her frown turns into a small smile. "I spit."

One morning much later, Caroline woke up and came into my room as is her custom. We went through our usual routine.

"Good morning, Caroline."

"Morning, Mommy."

"Did you sleep well?" I ask and so on.

"Love you, Mommy," she says. She speaks in her soft, morning voice.

"I love you, Caroline."

Then she yells, "I love you Mommy!" I'm caught off guard, not sure what to make of her yell. I fake-yell it back to her.

She mimics me, frustrated. "Don't say," and she whispers, "I love you. Say," and she yells, "I LOVE YOU!"

So I do. "I LOVE YOU Caroline!" I yell.

We look at each other, then smile. We do it again. I'm wearing polka dot satin, she's in pink Old Navy knit that clings to her tiny frame, and we stand barefoot on the cold stone bathroom floor yelling our love to each other, grinning.

Is the volume to convince me? To convince herself? Perhaps we are making up for the spots in our hearts where a well-bonded connection has been missing. Or maybe just loose.

Instead of tightly formed, well fitted, solid, stable love, our hearts are love-you-to-the-moon-and-back full, with little jiggly places that sometimes surprise us and grow less jiggly. So we chink the spaces with whatever we find in the moment, we stuff little yelling love rituals into the wobbly spots. And we smile, both a little more solid.

I don't remember what we said, just what it felt like to walk under towering old-growth cottonwood trees along an old river bottom remade into a bike path, the late afternoon sky blue and the day warm, Tim holding my hand.

I had wondered, as some would advise, if it might be best to keep a reserve of my weakness to myself, revealing only the deepest insecurities, vulnerabilities, to God, trying to salvage a scrap of a show of strength or dignity. To a degree we do that anyway because who but God can know who we are in our deepest recesses? We were mostly silent as we walked, taking and giving comfort from our nearness. How does he do this? I wondered.

We walked along the bike path and I listened to the dull thud on concrete the heels of his boots made as only his weight in them and his long stride could sound, as familiar to me as the sound of my breath, and I was as comforted as I was fifteen months ago when that sound and the man they carried rounded the corner on polished linoleum making my day. The cavalry was still at my side. And the cavalry was strong enough to handle raw weaknesses of body and soul.

"What a week we're having," we say and smile.

One evening I opened the windows in my office and the cool breeze drifted in as I walked to my desk and sat down; I moved aside my book *Brainlash* and pulled the testing report from underneath it where it had lain untouched for weeks.

I fingered this black-and-white proof that I am a woman in

possession of limitations and a meltdown and questions enough to fill the sky. Of things lost. A woman gone missing. Please take care of me. I have five children now. With this ring I thee wed, in sickness and in health. If I should die before I wake I will have done everything possible to be found.

On the shelf above my desk were piles of books I'd been reading ever since a friend had told me about a book on narrative nonfiction and I'd bought it immediately realizing this was the kind of writing I'd begun back at the beginning of my career before I knew there was a name for it or that it would be the work I loved, a way of doing something that made me feel most alive. Truth; beginning, middle, and end.

My first weekend at the Nieman Conference on Narrative Journalism at Harvard had sealed the deal and been the place I'd found my compass. I'd walked into a ballroom and stopped for a moment looking at the hundreds of journalists who loved true story as much as I did. These are my people, I thought. I felt the same way when I began some public radio and audio documentary work. Who I was a long time ago is who I am now. There's no need to choose between what feels expected and what feels true.

The great thing about finding one's compass is that it helps you find your way.

Leaning against my compass books on the eye-level shelf above my desk was my black Moleskine notebook, the elastic slightly stretched and the edges of the cover worn. One page was dog-eared and highlighted and starred at a phrase I'd written that had changed me:

Know who you are and be that.

I am a woman in possession of a miracle, even one missed, and I am a storyteller telling tales that are true.

I opened my file drawer and tucked the testing report in a manila folder, gently burying it in the back, and shut the drawer, solid, soft, closed, then I picked up *Brainlash* and walked to my bookshelf and slid it on the bottom shelf. My Moleskine gem took its place.

I walked into Caroline's room and pulled her onto my lap in the yellow slip-covered Dream. She was scrubbed and smelled of Johnson's baby shampoo and strawberry body wash, a blend of baby and big girl that she was becoming, her damp curls clinging to her head. I reached for a book on the white Shabby Chic bookshelf. A white sad-faced dog with a cheery bird on his head looked at me from the turquoise cover.

I opened to the first page of the story and read how the mother bird sat on her egg until the baby bird came out, I read how the baby bird didn't see his mother, I read how the baby bird wanted to find her. Caroline grinned. I hesitated, then read on. The baby bird had to find his mother, I told her, but since he didn't know where she was, he wondered if he even had a mother.

I patted her, and rocked us in the chair, and thought how much I'd wanted to survive and to find the meaning in the struggle, but how getting peace and redemption and the staggeringly beautiful transcendence of love was more than enough.

We got to the part of the story where the baby bird cried out that he wanted his mother, as every baby does. "Just then the mother bird came back to the tree . . . 'Do you know who I am?' she said to her baby," I read, stroking her soft, still round cheek, rocking away, and the baby did. "'You are my mother!'"

I looked down at my little girl. "Did the baby have a mother, Caroline?"

She nodded. "Yes."

I thought of the file folders on my desk filled with my reporting notes for the stories in progress and the ones to come, interviews with people where I'd ask questions and their stories fall out that I get the privilege of catching. Beginning, middle, and end.

"Know who you are and be that!" I whispered, the words I'd said when I was lost no more, when I remembered who I was.

"The end," I said, closing the book. We looked at each other and smiled. Then together, we got out of the chair.

Epilogue

In October after that summer Jacquelyn put on white satin and Noah Ayers slid a band of gold on her finger. We all burst out of the white-spired Air Force Academy chapel and into the reception, glowing with strings of sparkly white lights, vanilla candles, tangerine calla lilies in clear glass vases, and so many people we loved. Tim toasted, the small orchestra played, the bride and groom danced, and I absorbed the joy. Seemed like everyone in this room had helped us three years ago. The dance floor filled and Tim took me in his arms, we beamed at each other as we danced.

"I can't stop thinking that this is everyone who would have been at your . . ."

"I know," I said. "Me too."

"I'm so glad you didn't miss this," he said, leaning his chin on my forehead while our children danced around us.

The wedding had come after a summer and autumn of rest and healing following that spring's crisis, a healing no less important than the prior healing, albeit less spectacular. I sought and received good medical care for specific issues that had been discovered, sleep returned gradually, which when severely compromised and then is recovered has the power to pretty much solve world peace. I gave myself, and my family gave me, time to adjust to new limitations and a life changed since August 30th, time to heal, body and soul. A few hiccups linger, limitations, intermittent pain, some remaining post-ARDS issues, souvenirs of my journey, because life won't be the same as before.

One morning a few days ago as I write this I stood in our bathroom telling Tim about some of my cognitive struggles. "So," he says, "what you're telling me is you have a brain cloud."

I burst into laughter at the Tom Hanks' movie line in *Joe Versus the Volcano*.

"Exactly," I say. "But remember what Joe said when he faced his brain cloud while he was adrift on the sea and his love lay unconscious? Remember?"

"I forgot."

I tell him how Joe was about to die. If not from the brain cloud, then because they were floating on luggage in the middle of the sea. The moon rose huge in the sky. He dropped to his knees on the raft and lifted his arms like he was embracing the moon, and he said, "Thank you, God, for giving me another day of life."

We laugh; I am no longer winter; he is still the warmth of a hundred summer days.

One night years after my experience, right after the Haiti earthquake devastated Port-au-Prince, I drove down I-25 in Denver listening to a Colorado Public Radio interview. A man named James Gulley described how he had endured five days under the rubble of the Montana hotel that had collapsed in the quake. He'd been trapped in a five-foot-high space with five colleagues for five days, until French rescuers heard them. He told of singing and prayer, darkness and hope, and pain; two of his colleagues did not survive the ordeal. I listened to his extraordinary tale, captivated. Then, there it was. The question. The interviewer asked him, "What did you learn?" It struck me that he was being asked this question when he had only been rescued a few days earlier. How much can we possibly fully understand the meaning of what may be a singular unprecedented life event only days after experiencing it?

He hesitated. I turned the radio up. Two seconds of silence, then this:

"Well, I think it's easy to spout platitudes about 'Wow, God saved my life.' Well, he didn't save the lives of my two colleagues. I can't answer theologically the question of why my life was spared and the lives of my friends were not spared. I can't answer the question of why the lives of thousands and thousands of Haitians have been lost. It's not about being favored. There's always a mystery there as to why one person is more fortunate than another. All one can do is say I have been given a gift. A new gift of life. And all I can do is use that gift in the best way possible. Not selfishly for myself but for the sake of other people. And . . . I will do it not only because I've gotten that life, but for the sake of those who didn't get that life as well."

I listened to his astounding answer and wanted to pull over to the shoulder of the highway and weep. That's it. That's it, I thought—use the gift; offer it up, offer it out. Live well, live grateful, forever.

Claire, Collin, and Allison have grown and begun their own adventure called life and Noah and Jacquelyn had their first baby, Eloise Allison Ayers; Jacquelyn is a sister-mother no more.

When Caroline was almost six I packed a pink rolling suitcase small enough for her to navigate and a backpack with Millicent, her stuffed dog, sticking out the top. She wore her backpack and pulled her own suitcase and we navigated through airports and marble-floored train stations. Riding on one train I turned to Caroline.

"Have you ever walked through a train while it's moving?" I asked, knowing otherwise as this was her maiden train trip.

"No! Will they let us do that?"

"Let's go," and we walked through a couple of cars, watching the ground stream by through the cracks between cars, until we got to the club car.

"Here you are, Miss Caro. Potato chips for you, fruit of the vine for me."

"Thanks, Mommy. Mommy? This is fun."

"Caroline, you have the soul of a traveler. We are simpatico."
"What's that mean?"
"It means you and I . . . travel well together."
When we returned home and went out for a mother-daughter spaghetti dinner with maps of the world and Thailand on the table. I asked her, pennies and bodies pending, "Where would you want to travel next?"
"To Maine. Or China," she said. We clinked ice water to that. I wondered if I'd ever read to her about Jonah and the fish's belly, if we'd talked about how good it is, after traveling, to come home.

A few weeks later I stepped off a plane in Bangkok with my passport, Thailand map, notebooks, and radio recording gear stowed in my backpack. At the Thai-Myanmar border I slept in a refugee camp to report on Burmese people from the Karen tribe who had been displaced after fleeing the oppression from military government, then I traveled down-country and into a jungle where a woman and her husband gathered people broken from conflict and war; the mentally ill, old and infirm, and the young, orphans.

The afternoon was hot and the air thick and steamy as I walked up the hill on the compound to talk with more people who were eager to share what it was like to be them. I stopped for a moment to catch my breath and then stood still on the trail, happy, in wonder. Their stories fell out and I had the privilege of catching them.

At the end of the day I climbed into the van with the people who'd brought us and slid across the middle seat, legs sticking to hot vinyl as I checked my recordings and notes, the gold of true stories people wanted told, and wiped sweat dripping down my back and leaned back, spent. A woman with us turned to me and said, "I wouldn't want to do what you're doing for anything."

I looked at her and smiled. I had been lost, then found, then lost again. I'd found a love gone missing, and now I was lost no longer. Know who you are and be that.

Author's Note

Besides living this story, writing it was surreal. Reporting it was like uncovering a story about someone else. It involved me, yet for much of it, I wasn't there, so I reported it just as I do when I write a piece of literary journalism or narrative nonfiction about another person. A strange experience indeed.

The memoir genre sparks discussions about veracity. Most everyone agrees they should never be made-up, lies. Call that fiction instead. But there are different stances toward how they are written. Some believe emotional truth matters most and don't mind embellishment or looseness with facts, while others feel factual truth is paramount (if the author says there is a horse, there should have been an actual horse). "Strict constructionists" on one end, "just give me the essence" on the other, and lots of approaches in between. There's no one right way (other than the "lie" thing). I like reported memoir, both reading and writing it, and I've tried to be as true to both essence and fact as possible. Here are my reporting methods:

Dialogue is in quote marks even though it's only as close to accurate as I can get, not verbatim. There are no composite characters and all names except one are real. Much of the dialogue and all of the internal thoughts of other characters came from the dozens of people I interviewed. For some scenes, I cross-referenced the hundreds of pages of transcripts from those recordings and other documents. I went back to some of the locations I wrote about and took some details from photographs, diaries, medical records, weather records, video, my notes, others' emails, and Tim's updates written at the time of the events.

What, and why, and how accurately do we remember something? How does someone else remember it? There will be mistakes and differences in how people remember events, but such is the watery flow of memory. Not to mention the watery nature of a coma.

Acknowledgments

Thank you, to . . .

The caregivers, doctors, and medical team who saved my life. Dr. Fenton—thank you for helping to keep me breathing. And to South Denver Pulmonary.

Tim—I can't imagine a man loving more purely and self-sacrificially than you. You are a good man, one who lives out your sense of duty, seeing it only as love. Thank you for sheltering and leading our children with quiet strength, for being my advocate, and for loving me in my weakness, failures, the good and the grace.

My children, Jacquelyn, Claire, Collin, Allison, Noah, and Caro—you know how to love each other and your dad and me like nothing I've ever seen. You lived what family is all about. Thank you forever.

My dear friends who helped hold together my family, hold up Tim, and hold onto me: Kathy and Tom Groom, Susan Wilkinson, and Brenda Koinis.

Paul and Barbara Britton, Donna and Greg Patchell, and the Britton clan—family extraordinaire.

When there is an army of people who do something as amazing as what was done for my family and me, for so long, it is impossible to name everyone—there would be hundreds. To the prayer army around the world (literally) and everyone who helped us (seen or unseen), you have my deepest and life-long gratitude and humble thanks. Heritage Evangelical Free Church—as one nurse told my friend Coletta, she'd never seen people come around a family like that. You're an example of a church who got it right. Wow, do you people know how to love.

Especially Brent and Sharon Kinman, Craig and Coletta Smith, Kevin and Carol Mackey, Denise and Jeff Chang, Becky and Greg Johnson, Jeff and Amy Benge, Barb Larsen, Sharon Lindsey, Sue Weinroth, Jaynee Hodgkins, Jack Johnson, Rod and Beth Claussen, and Greg and Renee Ruff.

Erica Good—can I keep you as my research and author's assistant forever?

Tim's associates at Archstone who martialed many meals, and the Advanced Writers and Speakers Association—what generosity!

Lonnie Hull DuPont, Twila Bennett, Michele Misiak, Barb Barnes, Erin Bartels, Dave Lewis, and perhaps the most long-suffering publishing team in history. Thank you for continuing to wait for and champion this book for so long. I'm honored.

The ARDS Foundation—thank you, Eileen Rubin, for creating it. You educate, support, and give hope to patients and their families affected by ARDS. And for your fund-raising for research. (Ardsusa.org is a goldmine.)

The Nieman Foundation for Journalism at Harvard University, and the Center for Documentary Studies at Duke University—thank you for the tools and so much inspiration. Stories matter; life is happening, document it. Right?

And Caroline—I love you with my whole heart, to the moon and back.

Notes

1. Patricia Hampl, *The Florist's Daughter* (New York: Mariner, 2009), 47.
2. Ibid., 48.
3. Elizabeth Gilbert, *Eat, Pray, Love* (New York: Penguin, 2007), 93–94.
4. Isaiah 43:2 NIV.
5. Frederick Buechner, *The Magnificent Defeat* (New York: HarperCollins, 1985), 47.
6. Joan Didion, *The Year of Magical Thinking* (New York: Vintage, 2007), 44.
7. The following excerpts taken from Gail L. Denton, *Brainlash: Maximize Your Recovery from Mild Brain Injury* (New York: Demos Medical Publishing, 1999).

Lindsey O'Connor is an author, freelance journalist, and speaker who has contributed to public radio's *Weekend America*, WashingtonPost.com, *The Rocky Mountain News*, *Christianity Today*, *Writer's Digest*, *Guideposts*, and others. She has reported internationally, is a former broadcaster, was a finalist for an Audie Award, and is a member of The Association of Independents in Radio and the American Society of Journalists and Authors. She and her family live in Colorado.

—·—— *Connect with* ——·—

LINDSEY O'CONNOR

LINDSEYOCONNOR.COM

 : LindseyOConnor

 : Lindsey OConnor